MINNESOTA EMPLOYMENT & CONSUMER LAWYERS & LAW

LEADING AMERICAN
ATTORNEYS

America's Most Respected Legal Counsel As Selected By Their Peers

Published 1997

The publisher would like to thank John Wendt of the University of St. Thomas for writing the "Sports Law" section. The publisher would also like to thank Leading Minnesota Attorneys Daniel J. Heuel of Muir, Heuel, Carlson & Spelhaug, P.A.; Donald E. Horton of Horton and Associates; Gerald T. Laurie of Lapp, Laurie, Libra, Abramson & Thomson, Chartered; and Clarence A. Anderson, supervising reemployment judge with the Minnesota Department of Economic Security for reviewing and editing "Employment Law: Individual" chapter.

ISBN: 1-885573-25-1

LEADING AMERICAN ATTORNEYS
527 MARQUETTE AVENUE, SUITE 2100
MINNEAPOLIS, MN 55402
Phone: (612) 904-3200
Fax: (612) 904-3288
E-Mail: staff@lawlead.com
Web Site: http://www.lawlead.com

PURPOSE:

The purpose of the *Minnesota Employment & Consumer Lawyers & Law Guide* is to provide consumers with the legal information they need and the names of reputable and qualified Minnesota attorneys who can help.

TABLE OF CONTENTS

EXTENSIVE EXPERIENCE INDEX

In the context of Consumer Law, the following attorneys have extensive experience in the specific areas indicated below. For a more complete description of their experience and credentials, see their individual biographical profile on the pages indicated.

LOCATION BY AREA OF LAW INDEX

The following Leading American Attorneys are listed by area of law and geographic location. Those with biographical profiles can be found on the page number following the attorney's name.

Arts, Entertainment & Sports Law

Minneapolis	Abdo, Kenneth J.	(612) 333-1526	30
Minneapolis	Danielson, Laura J.	(612) 349-5767	. . . . .31, 124
Minneapolis	Gislason, Barbara J.	(612) 331-8033	32
Minneapolis	Satorius, Daniel M.	(612) 333-1526	33
Minneapolis	Tanick, Marshall H.	(612) 339-4295	67

Bankruptcy Law: Individual

Minneapolis	Ball, Ian Traquair	(612) 338-1313	
New Brighton	Prescott, Jack L.	(612) 633-2757	42
St. Paul	Iannacone, Michael L.	(612) 224-3361	41

Employment Law: Individual

Alexandria	Dolan, Michael J.	(320) 762-2361	95
Alexandria	Lervick, John C.	(320) 763-3141	
Anoka	Bolt, David M.	(612) 427-8888	
Bemidji	McKay, Susan A.	(218) 759-9688	60
Bloomington	Villaume, Philip G.	(612) 851-0823	. . . . , , 68, 110
Duluth	Burns, Richard R.	(218) 722-4706	
Duluth	Bye, Don L.	(218) 628-0940	52
Fargo	Maring, David S.	(701) 237-5297	
Fergus Falls	Kershner, H. Morrison (Morrie)	(218) 736-5493	
Fergus Falls	Pemberton, Richard L.	(218) 736-5493	
Little Falls	Anderson, Douglas P.	(320) 632-5458	
Mankato	Maschka, Gerald L.	(507) 387-3002	
Minneapolis	Anderson, Jeffrey P.	(612) 338-1919	
Minneapolis	Bloom, Michael B.	(612) 333-5831	
Minneapolis	Boler, Jean M.	(612) 871-8910	
Minneapolis	Borene Scott M.	(612) 321-0082	123
Minneapolis	Cooper, Stephen W.	(612) 332-9002	53
Minneapolis	Gislason, Barbara J.	(612) 331-8033	32
Minneapolis	Horton, Donald E.	(612) 831-6900	56
Minneapolis	Kaster, James H.	(612) 338-1919	57
Minneapolis	Laurie, Gerald, T.	(612) 338-5815	58
Minneapolis	Mavity, William J.	(612) 339-3001	59
Minneapolis	Miller, Nancy	(612) 333-5831	61
Minneapolis	Nichols, Donald H.	(612) 338-1919	63
Minneapolis	O'Brien, Maurice W "Bill"	(612) 333-5831	64
Minneapolis	Ryan, James G.	(612) 630-0010	65
Minneapolis	Tanick, Marshall H.	(612) 339-4295	67
Minneapolis	Weissman, Gary A.	(612) 337-9519	
Minneapolis	Wicka, James C.	(612) 672-3668	111
Rochester	Heuel, Daniel J.	(507) 288-4110	55
Rochester	Wendland, Craig W.	(507) 288-5440	
St. Louis Park	Corwin, Gregg M.	(612) 544-7774	54

St. Paul	Anderson, Jeffrey R.	(612) 227-9990	51
St. Paul	Mattos, Patricia G.	(612) 698-8841	125
St. Paul	McAdoo, Barbara (Bobbi)	(612) 523-2068	
St. Paul	Mullen, Joanne J.	(612) 227-9990	62
St. Paul	Snyder, Stephen J.	(612) 290-8400	66
Thief River Falls	Marben, Kurt J.	(218) 681-4002	
Wadena	Kennedy, Charles R.	(218) 631-2505	
Woodbury	Sawicki, Walter E.	(612) 730-6900	
Worthington	Malters, James E.	(507) 376-4166	

Felony & Misdemeanor Criminal Defense

Alexandria	Dolan, Michael J.	(320) 762-2361	95
Bemidji	McKay, Susan A.	(218) 759-9688	60
Bloomington	Mohr, Gordon G.	(612) 831-8700	102
Bloomington	Villaume, Philip G.	(612) 851-0823	. . . . .68, 110
Cloquet	Belfry, K. Scott	(218) 878-0672	87
Cloquet	Newby, Harry L., Jr.	(218) 879-3331	
Detroit Lakes	Thorwaldsen, Paul R.	(218) 847-5646	108
Duluth	Keegan, David C.	(218) 722-7813	97
Grand Rapids	Undem, John Drake	(218) 326-0321	109
Mankato	Blethen, Bailey W.	(507) 345-1166	88
Mankato	Bluth, Joseph P.	(507) 387-5661	89
Mankato	Manahan, James H.	(507) 387-5661	100
Minneapolis	Bauer, Thomas E.	(612) 337-9555	86
Minneapolis	Birrell, Andrew S.	(612) 871-7000	
Minneapolis	Bruno, Frederic	(612) 545-7900	90
Minneapolis	Caplan, Allan Hart	(612) 341-4570	92
Minneapolis	Colich, Michael J.	(612) 333-7007	94
Minneapolis	Cooper, Stephen W.	(612) 332-9002	53
Minneapolis	Goldfarb, Stephen M.	(612) 546-8888	
Minneapolis	Kelley, Douglas A.	(612) 371-9090	
Minneapolis	Lee, John M.	(612) 371-9090	
Minneapolis	Mauzy, William J.	(612) 340-9108	101
Minneapolis	Meshbesher, Ronald I.	(612) 339-9121	
Minneapolis	Mohs, Daniel M.	(612) 591-1616	102
Minneapolis	Rapoport, Larry G.	(612) 825-2331	
Minneapolis	Ring, Jeffrey B.	(612) 797-7464	104
Minneapolis	Roston, David G.	(612) 332-3100	105
Minneapolis	Sheehy, John P.	(612) 339-9121	106
Minneapolis	Shiah, Thomas H.	(612) 338-0066	107
Minneapolis	Wernick, Mark S.	(612) 871-8456	111
Rochester	Lund, Kevin A.	(507) 288-9122	98
St. Cloud	Eller, Daniel A.	(320) 253-3700	96
St. Paul	Ayers, David L.	(612) 222-8400	85
St. Paul	Cleary, Edward J.	(612) 296-3952	93
St. Paul	Malone, Robert G.	(612) 227-6549	99
Wayzata	Cahill, Peter A.	(612) 449-9822	91

Immigration Law: Individual

Minneapolis	Borene, Scott M.	(612) 321-0082	123
Minneapolis	Danielson, Laura J.	(612) 349-5767	. . . . .31, 124
Minneapolis	McIvor, Saiko Y.	(612) 321-0082	126
St. Paul	Mattos, Patricia G.	(612) 698-8841	125

ADDRESS LISTINGS BY AREA OF LAW INDEX

The following Leading American Attorneys are listed by area of law. Those with biographical profiles can be found on the page number following the attorney's name.

Arts, Entertainment & Sports Law

Abdo, Kenneth J. - *Abdo & Abdo, P.A.* 30
710 Northstar West - 625 Marquette Avenue - Minneapolis, MN 55402
Phone: (612) 333-1526, Fax: (612) 342-2608
Danielson, Laura J. - *Patterson & Keough, P.A.* 31, 124
1200 Rand Tower - 527 Marquette Avenue South - Minneapolis, MN 55402
Phone: (612) 349-5767, Fax: (612) 349-9266, 800· (800) 331-4537,
E-mail: 1jd@pklaw.com
Gislason, Barbara J. - *Barbara J. Gislason & Associates* 32
506 St. Anthony Main   219 SE Main Street - Minneapolis, MN 55414
Phone: (612) 331-8033, Fax: (612) 331-8115
Satorius, Daniel M. - *Abdo & Abdo, P.A.* 33
710 Northstar West - 625 Marquette Avenue - Minneapolis, MN 55402
Phone: (612) 333-1526, Fax: (612) 342-2608
Tanick, Marshall H. - *Mansfield & Tanick, P.A.* 67
1560 International Centre - 900 Second Avenue South
Minneapolis, MN 55402-3383
Phone: (612) 339-4295, Fax: (612) 339-3161, E-mail: tanick@mansfieldtanick.com,
Web Site: www.mansfieldtanick.com

Bankruptcy Law: Individual

Ball, Ian Traquair - *Attorney at Law*
1111 Third Avenue South, Suite 351 - Minneapolis, MN 55404
Phone: (612) 338-1313
Iannacone, Michael J. - *Iannacone Law Office* 41
101 East Fifth Street, Suite 1614 - St. Paul, MN 55101
Phone: (612) 224-3361, Fax: (612) 297-6187
Prescott, Jack L. - *Prescott & Pearson, P.A.* 42
403 Eighth Avenue NW - P.O. Box 120088 - New Brighton, MN 55112
Phone: (612) 633-2757, Fax: (612) 633-7562

Employment Law: Individual

Anderson, Douglas P. - *Rosenmeier Anderson & Vogel*
210 Second Street NE - Little Falls, MN 56345
Phone: (320) 632-5458, Fax: (320) 632-5496
Anderson, Jeffrey P. - *Nichols Kaster & Anderson*
4644 IDS Center - 80 South Eighth Street - Minneapolis, MN 55402-2242
Phone: (612) 338-1919, Fax: (612) 338-4878, E-mail: anderson@nka.com,
Web Site: www.nka.com
Anderson, Jeffrey R. - *Reinhardt & Anderson* 51
1000 E. First National Bank Building - 332 Minnesota Street - St. Paul, MN 55101
Phone: (612) 227-9990, Fax: (612) 297-6543

Bloom, Michael B. - *Miller • O'Brien • Bloom*
1208 Plymouth Building - 12 South Sixth Street
Minneapolis, MN 55402-1529
Phone: (612) 333-5831, Fax: (612) 342-2613, E-mail: mbloom@m-o-b.com
Boler, Jean M. - *Sprenger & Lang*
325 Ridgewood Avenue - Minneapolis, MN 55403
Phone: (612) 871-8910, Fax: (612) 871-9270,
E-mail: sprenger_mn@worldnet.att.net
Bolt, David M. - *Soucie, Buchman, Grover & Bolt, Ltd.*
2150 Third Avenue North, Suite 100 - Anoka, MN 55303-2200
Phone: (612) 427-8888, Fax: (612) 421-2560, 800: (800) 499-2394,
E-mail: info@sbgb-law.com, Web Site: sbgb-law.com
Borene, Scott M. - *Borene Law Firm, P.A. - Immigration Law Group* 123
4602 IDS Center - Minneapolis, MN 55402
Phone: (612) 321-0082, Fax: (612) 332-8368
Burns, Richard R. - *Hanft, Fride, O'Brien, Harries, Swelbar & Burns, P.A.*
1000 First Bank Place - 130 West Superior Street - Duluth, MN 55802-2094
Phone: (218) 722-4766, Fax: (218) 720-4920
Bye, Don L. - *Don L. Bye, P.A.* 52
2802 West First Street - Duluth, MN 55806
Phone: (218) 628-0940, Fax: (218) 628-0889
Cooper, Stephen W. - *The Cooper Law Firm, Chartered* 53
4747 First Bank Place - 602 Second Avenue South - Minneapolis, MN 55402
Phone: (612) 332-9002, Fax: (612) 332-4903
Corwin, Gregg M. - *Gregg M. Corwin & Associates* 54
1660 South Highway 100 - Suite 508 East - St. Louis Park, MN 55416-1534
Phone: (612) 544-7774, Fax: (612) 544-7151
Dolan, Michael J. - *Thornton, Hegg, Reif, Johnston & Dolan, P.A.* 95
1017 Broadway - P.O. Box 819 - Alexandria, MN 56308-0819
Phone: (320) 762-2361, Fax: (320) 762-1638,
E-mail: thrjd@alexandria.polaristel.net
Gislason, Barbara J. - *Barbara J. Gislason & Associates* 32
506 St. Anthony Main - 219 SE Main Street - Minneapolis, MN 55414
Phone: (612) 331-8033, Fax: (612) 331-8115
Heuel, Daniel J. - *Muir, Heuel, Carlson & Spelhaug, P.A.* 55
404 Marquette Bank Building - P.O. Box 1057 - Rochester, MN 55903
Phone: (507) 288-4110, Fax: (507) 288-4122, 800: (800) 282-4110
Horton, Donald E. - *Horton and Associates* 56
4930 West 77th Street, Suite 210 - Minneapolis, MN 55435-4804
Phone: (612) 831-6900, Fax: (612) 893-3126,
E-mail: horton@winternet.com, Web Site: www.hortonlaw.com
Kaster, James H. - *Nichols Kaster & Anderson* 57
4644 IDS Center - 80 South Eighth Street - Minneapolis, MN 55402-2242
Phone: (612) 338-1919, Fax: (612) 338-4878, Web Site: www.nka.com
Kennedy, Charles R. - *Kennedy, Nervig & Carlisle, L.L.P.*
503 South Jefferson Street - Wadena, MN 56482
Phone: (218) 631-2505, Fax: (218) 631-9078
Kershner, H. Morrison (Morrie) - *Pemberton, Sorlie, Sefkow, Rufer & Kershner, P.L.L.P.*
110 North Mill Street - P.O. Box 866 - Fergus Falls, MN 56538-0866
Phone: (218) 736-5493, Fax: (218) 736-3950, 800: (800) 862-3651,
E-mail: kershner@thecomputerplace.com
Laurie, Gerald T. - *Lapp, Laurie, Libra, Abramson & Thomson, Chartered* 58
One Financial Plaza, Suite 1800 - 120 South Sixth Street
Minneapolis, MN 55402
Phone: (612) 338-5815, Fax: (612) 338-6651

Lervick, John C. - *Swenson, Lervick, Syverson & Anderson, Ltd.*
710 Broadway - Box 787 - Alexandria, MN 56308
Phone: (320) 763-3141, Fax: (320) 763-3657, E-mail: slsa@rea-alp.com
Malters, James E. - *Von Holtum, Malters & Shepherd*
607 Tenth Street - P.O. Box 517 - Worthington, MN 56187-0517
Phone: (507) 376-4166, Fax: (507) 376-6359, E-mail: jmalters@rconnect.com
Marben, Kurt J. - *Charlson, Marben & Jorgenson, P.A.*
119 West Second Street - P.O. Box 506 - Thief River Falls, MN 56701-0506
Phone: (218) 681-4002, Fax: (218) 681-4004
Maring, David S. - *Maring Williams Law Office*
1220 Main Avenue, Suite 105 - P.O. Box 2103 - Fargo, MN 58107-2103
Phone: (701) 237-5297, Fax: (701) 235-2268, 800: (800) 492-5297,
E-mail: maring@linkup.net
Maschka, Gerald L. - *Farrish, Johnson & Maschka, P.L.L.P.*
200 Union Square, Suite 200
201 North Broad Street - P.O. Box 550 - Mankato, MN 56002-0550
Phone: (507) 387-3002, Fax: (507) 625-4002, Web Site: www.fjm-law.com
Mattos, Patricia G. - *Attorney at Law* 125
Rowan Professional Building
1539 Grand Avenue - St. Paul, MN 55105
Phone: (612) 698-8841, Fax: (612) 698-5703
Mavity, William J. - *William J. Mavity & Associates* 59
2525 Metropolitan Centre
333 South Seventh Street - Minneapolis, MN 55402
Phone: (612) 339-3001, Fax: (612) 339-3267
McAdoo, Barbara (Bobbi) - *Dispute Resolution Institute*
Hamline University School of Law
1536 Hewitt Avenue - St. Paul, MN 55105
Phone: (612) 523-2068, Fax: (612) 641-2236,
E-mail: bmcadoo@seq.hamline.edu
McKay, Susan A - *McKay Law Office* 60
305 America Avenue - Bemidji, MN 56601
Phone: (218) 759-9688, Fax: (218) 759-9692, 800: (800) 640-9688,
E-mail: smckay@mail.paulbunyan.net
Miller, Nancy - *Miller • O'Brien • Bloom* 61
1208 Plymouth Building - 12 South Sixth Street
Minneapolis, MN 55402-1529
Phone: (612) 333-5831, Fax: (612) 342-2613, 800: (800) 850-8335,
E-mail: nmiller@m-o-b.com
Mullen, Joanne J. - *Reinhardt & Anderson* 62
1000 E. First National Bank Building - 332 Minnesota Street
St. Paul, MN 55101
Phone: (612) 227-9990, Fax: (612) 297-6543
Nichols, Donald H. - *Nichols Kaster & Anderson* 63
4644 IDS Center - 80 South Eighth Street - Minneapolis, MN 55402-2242
Phone: (612) 338-1919, Fax: (612) 338-4878, Web Site: www.nka.com
O'Brien, Maurice W. "Bill" - *Miller • O'Brien • Bloom* 64
1208 Plymouth Building - 12 South Sixth Street
Minneapolis, MN 55402-1529
Phone: (612) 333-5831, Fax: (612) 342-2613
Pemberton, Richard L. - *Pemberton, Sorlie, Sefkow, Rufer & Kershner, P.L.L.P.*
110 North Mill Street - P.O. Box 866 - Fergus Falls, MN 56538-0866
Phone: (218) 736-5493, Fax: (218) 736-3950, 800: (800) 862-3651
Ryan, James G. - *Attorney at Law* 65
3908 IDS Center - 80 South Eighth Street - Minneapolis, MN 55402
Phone: (612) 630-0010, Fax: (612) 630-0015

Sawicki, Walter E. - *Sawicki, Neese & Phelps, P.A.*
1811 Weir Drive, Suite 275 - Woodbury, MN 55125
Phone: (612) 730-6900, Fax: (612) 730-8110, 800: (800) 642-5076
Snyder, Stephen J. - *Winthrop & Weinstine, P.A.* 66
3200 Minnesota World Trade Center - 30 East Seventh Street
St. Paul, MN 55101
Phone: (612) 290-8400, Fax: (612) 292-9347
Tanick, Marshall H. - *Mansfield & Tanick, P.A.* 67
1560 International Centre - 900 Second Avenue South
Minneapolis, MN 55402-3383
Phone: (612) 339-4295, Fax: (612) 339-3161,
E-mail: tanick@mansfieldtanick.com, Web Site: www.mansfieldtanick.com
Villaume, Philip G. - *Philip G. Villaume & Associates* 68, 110
7900 International Drive, Suite 675 - Bloomington, MN 55425
Phone: (612) 851-0823, Fax: (612) 851-0824
Weissman, Gary A. - *Weissman Law Office*
701 Fourth Avenue South, Suite 500 - Minneapolis, MN 55415
Phone: (612) 337-9519, Fax: (612) 338-1771
Wendland, Craig W. - *Dingle & Wendland, Ltd.*
300 Norwest Center - P.O. Box 939 - Rochester, MN 55902
Phone: (507) 288-5440, Fax: (507) 281-8288
Wicka, James C. - *Messerli & Kramer, P.A.* 69
150 South Fifth Street - Suite 1800 - Minneapolis, MN 55402
Phone: (612) 672-3668, Fax: (612) 672-3777

Felony & Misdemeanor Criminal Defense

Ayers, David L. - *Ayers & Riehm* 85
Firstar Center, Suite 2330 - 101 East Fifth Street - St. Paul, MN 55101
Phone: (612) 222-8400, Fax: (612) 222-1844

Bauer, Thomas E. - *Thomas E. Bauer and Associates* 86
701 Fourth Avenue South, Suite 600 - Minneapolis, MN 55415-1633
Phone: (612) 337-9555, Fax: (612) 333-2701

Belfry, K. Scott - *Belfry Law Office, Chartered* 87
6 Thirteenth Street - Cloquet, MN 55720
Phone: (218) 878-0672, Fax: (218) 879-2065

Birrell, Andrew S. - *Birrell Dunlap & Ritts, Ltd.*
2450 Park Avenue - Minneapolis, MN 55404
Phone: (612) 871-7000, Fax: (612) 871-3215, 800: (800) 368-4529

Blethen, Bailey W. - *Blethen, Gage & Krause, PLLP* 88
127 South Second Street - P.O. Box 3049 - Mankato, MN 56002-3049
Phone: (507) 345-1166, Fax: (507) 345-8003

Bluth, Joseph P. - *Manahan & Bluth Law Office, Chartered* 89
416 South Front Street - P.O. Box 287 - Mankato, MN 56002-0287
Phone: (507) 387-5661, Fax: (507) 387-2111, E-mail: mb_law@ic.mankato.mn.us

Bruno, Frederic - *Frederic Bruno & Associates* 90
5500 Wayzata Boulevard, Suite 730 - Minneapolis, MN 55416
Phone: (612) 545-7900, Fax: (612) 545-0834, E-mail: bruno@brunolaw.com

Cahill, Peter A. - *Cahill Law Office* 91
150 South Broadway Avenue - Wayzata, MN 55391-1701
Phone: (612) 449-9822, Fax: (612) 449-0167, 800: (888) 449-9822
E-mail: CahillLaw@aol.com

Caplan, Allan Hart - *Allan Hart Caplan & Associates* 92
525 Lumber Exchange Building - 10 South Fifth Street
Minneapolis, MN 55402
Phone: (612) 341-4570, Fax: (612) 341-0507

Cleary, Edward J. - *Cleary Law Office* 93
25 Constitution Avenue, Suite 105 - 445 Minnesota Street
St. Paul, MN 55155
Phone: (612) 296-3952, Fax: (612) 297-5801

Colich, Michael J. - *Colich & Associates* 94
10 South Fifth Street, Suite 420 - Minneapolis, MN 55402
Phone: (612) 333-7007, Fax: (612) 333-0492

Cooper, Stephen W. - *The Cooper Law Firm, Chartered* 53
4747 First Bank Place - 602 Second Avenue South - Minneapolis, MN 55402
Phone: (612) 332-9002, Fax: (612) 332-4903

Dolan, Michael J. - *Thornton, Hegg, Reif, Johnston & Dolan, P.A.* 95
1017 Broadway - P.O. Box 819 - Alexandria, MN 56308-0819
Phone: (320) 762-2361, Fax: (320) 762-1638,
E-mail: thrjd@alexandria.polaristel.net

Eller, Daniel A. - *Eller Law Office* 96
925 First Street South - St. Cloud, MN 56302
Phone: (320) 253-3700, Fax: (320) 253-3105

Goldfarb, Stephen M. - *Goldfarb & Associates, P.A.*
4600 West 29th Street - Minneapolis, MN 55416-4066
Phone: (612) 546-8888, Fax: (612) 926-6667,
E-mail: stevegoldfarb@juno.com

Keegan, David C. - *Attorney at Law* 97
1400 Alworth Building - 306 West Superior Street - Duluth, MN 55802
Phone: (218) 722-7813, Fax: (218) 726-1220,
E-mail: dkeegan@cp.duluth.mn.us

Kelley, Douglas A. - *Douglas A. Kelley, P.A.*
Centre Village Offices, Suite 2530 - 431 South Seventh Street
Minneapolis, MN 55402-1855
Phone: (612) 371-9090, Fax: (612) 371-0574

Lee, John M. - *Douglas A. Kelley, P.A.*
Centre Village Offices, Suite 2530 - 431 South Seventh Street
Minneapolis, MN 55402-1855
Phone: (612) 371-9090, Fax: (612) 371-0574

Lund, Kevin A. - *Lund & Patterson* 98
Historic Kelly Building - 7 Fourth Street SE - Rochester, MN 55904
Phone: (507) 288-9122, Fax: (507) 288-7753

Malone, Robert G. - *Attorney at Law* 99
386 North Wabasha Street, Suite 780 - St. Paul, MN 55102
Phone: (612) 227-6549, Fax: (612) 224-6151

Manahan, James H. - *Manahan & Bluth Law Office, Chartered* 100
416 South Front Street - P.O. Box 287 - Mankato, MN 56002-0287
Phone: (507) 387-5661, Fax: (507) 387-2111,
E-mail: mb_law@ic.mankato.mn.us

Mauzy, William J. - *Mauzy Law Firm* 101
Norwest Center, Suite 2885 - 90 South Seventh Street
Minneapolis, MN 55402
Phone: (612) 340-9108, Fax: (612) 340-1628

McKay, Susan A. - *McKay Law Office* 60
305 America Avenue - Bemidji, MN 56601
Phone: (218) 759-9688, Fax: (218) 759-9692, 800: (800) 640-9688,
E-mail: smckay@mail.paulbunyan.net, Web Site:

Meshbesher, Ronald I. - *Meshbesher & Spence, Ltd.*
1616 Park Avenue South - Minneapolis, MN 55404
Phone: (612) 339-9121, Fax: (612) 339-9188, 800: (800) 274-1616

Mohr, Gordon G. (Jeff) - *Gordon G. (Jeff) Mohr Law Offices* 102
5001 West 80th Street, Suite 1020 - Southgate Office Building - Bloomington, MN 55417
Phone: (612) 831-8700, Fax: (612) 831-6625

Mohs, Daniel M. - *Daniel M. Mohs & Associates, Ltd.* 103
The Colonnade, Suite 1025 - 5500 Wayzata Boulevard - Minneapolis, MN 55416
Phone: (612) 591-1616, Fax: (612) 591-1653

Newby, Harry L., Jr. - *Newby, Lingren, Carlson & Skare, Ltd.*
1219 14th Street - P.O. Box 760 - Cloquet, MN 55720-0760
Phone: (218) 879-3331, Fax: (218) 879-3201, 800: (800) 742-3210

Rapoport, Larry G. - *Law Offices of Larry Rapoport, Ltd.*
3001 Hennepin Avenue South, Suite 309B - Minneapolis, MN 55408
Phone: (612) 825-2331, Fax: (612) 825-0061

Ring, Jeffrey B. - *Jeffrey B. Ring & Associates* 104
The Interchange Tower, Suite 1690 - 600 South Highway 169
Minneapolis, MN 55426
Phone: (612) 797-7464, Fax: (612) 797-9555, E-mail: ringjbrish@aol.com

Roston, David G. - *Segal & Roston* 105
250 Second Avenue South, Suite 225 - Minneapolis, MN 55401
Phone: (612) 332-3100, Fax: (612) 335-3578

Sheehy, John P. - *Meshbesher & Spence, Ltd.* 106
1616 Park Avenue South - Minneapolis, MN 55404
Phone: (612) 339-9121, Fax: (612) 339-9188, 800: (800) 274-1616

Shiah, Thomas H. - *Law Offices of Thomas H. Shiah, Ltd.* 107
701 Fourth Avenue South, Suite 1240 - Minneapolis, MN 55415
Phone: (612) 338-0066, Fax: (612) 337-9020, E-mail: shiah@skypoint.com

Thorwaldsen, Paul R. - *Thorwaldsen, Quam, Beeson, Malmstrom & Sorum* 108
1105 Highway 10 East - P.O. Box 1599 - Detroit Lakes, MN 56502-1599
Phone: (218) 847-5646, Fax: (218) 847-3950

Undem, John Drake - *Undem Law Office* 109
521 North Pokegama Avenue - P.O. Box 428 - Grand Rapids, MN 55744
Phone: (218) 326-0321, Fax: (218) 326-0248,
E-mail: undem@northernnet.com

Villaume, Philip G. - *Philip G. Villaume & Associates* 68, 110
7900 International Drive, Suite 675 - Bloomington, MN 55425
Phone: (612) 851-0823, Fax: (612) 851-0824

Wernick, Mark S. - *Wernick Law Office* 111
2520 Park Avenue South - Minneapolis, MN 55404
Phone: (612) 871-8456, Fax: (612) 871-4168

Immigration Law: Individual

Borene, Scott M. - *Borene Law Firm, P.A. - Immigration Law Group* 123
4602 IDS Center - Minneapolis, MN 55402
Phone: (612) 321-0082, Fax: (612) 332-8368

FIRM PROFILES INDEX

The following Leading American Attorney firms are listed alphabetically. Those with biographical firm profiles can be found on the page number following the firm's name.

RESEARCH METHODOLOGY

The selection of Leading Minnesota Attorneys is based on the premise that attorneys know attorneys best. Our research group used the four-step process described below to identify Minnesota's most respected legal counsel as selected by their peers.

Step One: Market Research

Using a wide variety of established sources of information about attorneys, our market research staff generated lists of prominent attorneys throughout Minnesota in each area of the law. We asked these prominent attorneys to identify other outstanding Minnesota Attorneys. This market research set the stage for the next research phase, a survey of Minnesota Bar members that resulted in a list of peer-nominated attorneys.

Step Two: Attorney Survey: Peer Nomination

Using both direct mail and telephone survey methods, we first surveyed each of the identified prominent attorneys and followed that with a survey of thousands of members of the Minnesota Bar. Each was asked: "If you had a friend or relative who needed an attorney with expertise in a specific area of law with which you could not assist, to whom in Minnesota would you refer him or her?" Attorneys responded by providing names of those attorneys to whom they do or would make referrals. These independent recommendations are considered nominations, and only those receiving multiple nominations in a specific practice area were considered for selection as Leading Minnesota Attorneys (many attorneys are nominated in more than one area of the law).

Step Three: Verification

Information about this peer-nominated group of attorneys was verified by contacting the nominated attorney and/or his or her firm directly. We checked the basics like name, firm name, address, etc., but more importantly verified that the nominated attorney practices in the area of law for which they were nominated. We also verified that all peer-nominated attorneys were currently licensed to practice in Minnesota and in good standing with the Minnesota Bar.

Step Four: Selection

This list of verified peer-nominees was then presented to our Leading Minnesota Attorneys Advisory Board for review. They were asked to identify possible omissions and, in some cases, point out attorneys on the list for reconsideration based upon verifiable circumstances. Multiple votes from members of the Advisory Board were required for attorneys to be added or deleted from the list of verified nominees.

The Result

This four-step process resulted in a list of fewer than 6 percent of Minnesota's attorneys covering the breadth of practice areas and with appropriate geographic distribution throughout the state.

LEADING MINNESOTA ATTORNEYS ADVISORY BOARD

Leading Minnesota Attorneys wishes to thank the members of its Advisory Board. We sought a Board comprised of those attorneys held in the highest esteem by their peers and that was a well-balanced group in terms of geography and area of law practiced. All are of tremendous assistance in the development of the programs and services we offer and in reviewing the research process and selection of Leading Minnesota Attorneys.

ARTS & ENTERTAINMENT LAW

Kenneth J. Abdo	Abdo & Abdo, P.A.
Barbara J. Gislason	Barbara J. Gislason & Associates
John H. Stout	Fredrikson & Byron, P.A.

BANKRUPTCY LAW: INDIVIDUAL

Ian Ball	Attorney at Law
James Dailey	Dailey Law Office
Michael J. Iannacone	Iannacone Law Office
Jack L. Prescott	Prescott & Pearson, P.A.

EMPLOYMENT LAW: INDIVIDUAL

Daniel J. Heuel	Muir, Heuel, Carlson & Spelhaug, P.A.
Gerald T. Laurie	Lapp, Laurie, Libra, Abramson & Thomson, Chartered
William J. Mavity	William J. Mavity & Associates
Don H. Nichols	Nichols Kaster & Anderson
Maurice W. "Bill" O'Brien	Miller • O'Brien • Bloom
Marshall H. Tanick	Mansfield & Tanick, P.A.

FELONY & MISDEMEANOR CRIMINAL DEFENSE LAW

Joseph P. Bluth	Manahan & Bluth Law Office, Chartered
Frederic Eric Bruno	Fredric Bruno & Associates
Michael J. Colich	Colich & Associates
Daniel A. Eller	Eller Law Office
David C. Keegan	Keegan Law Office
Kevin A. Lund	Lund & Patterson
William J. Mauzy	Mauzy Law Firm

IMMIGRATION LAW: INDIVIDUAL

Scott M. Borene	Borene Law Firm, P.A.
Laura J. Danielson	Patterson & Keough, P.A.
Patricia G. Mattos	Attorney at Law
Howard S. Myers	Myers Thompson, P.A.

HOW TO SELECT AN ATTORNEY

Perhaps the first question for anyone reading this *Guide* is, "Do I have a legal problem and if so, do I need a lawyer?" America's legal system provides methods by which many of society's transactions are structured and maintained and through which disputes are resolved. Not every matter is a legal issue and the simplest way to find out whether the legal system can help solve your problem is to consult an attorney.

But which attorney? Lawyers differ in many ways. Choosing the right attorney is extremely important. The wrong choice can be both expensive and frustrating. You should be prudent and research your decision carefully.

The three-step process described below involves preparing a list of potential attorneys for consideration, researching their background and experience and then interviewing those most likely to be suitable. This *Guide* can assist you greatly in selecting the correct attorney by providing names and addresses of Leading Attorneys, as well as several biographical profiles.

STEP 1: PREPARE A LIST

The first step in choosing a lawyer is to generate a list of potential prospects. This can be done by noting advertisements for lawyers, asking friends, associates, other attorneys or professionals for the names of attorneys they know or by contacting a referral service for a recommendation.

Each attorney whose name appears in this *Guide* was selected by his or her peers as someone to whom they would send a friend or relative in need of legal assistance. Selection by their peers is a powerful endorsement of their capabilities and, in combination with names you may obtain from other sources, the list of Leading Attorneys contained in this *Guide* should provide ample options for your selection process.

STEP 2: RESEARCH THE ATTORNEYS ON THE LIST

Some of the most important issues to research and consider about the lawyers on your list include the items below.

REPUTATION

An attorney's reputation for technical skill is important, but only you can determine its relevance to a particular legal matter. Savvy individuals with a variety of legal concerns often employ different lawyers to work on different matters because they realize no lawyer can be all things to all people and handle every type of legal question.

As important as a lawyer's technical reputation is, his or her ethical reputation may be even more important. It pays to ask around about a lawyer's ethical reputation, for a lawyer's reputation is well known among other professionals. To find out about the reputation of an attorney you are considering, ask for references from past clients, ask other attorneys about the lawyer, and check with the state bar to determine if there have been any ethical or other problems associated with this attorney. Lawyers should be willing to provide references or a list of past clients whom the prospective client can contact. Beware of lawyers with poor ethical reputations.

EXPERIENCE AND SPECIALIZATION

Because it is wise to hire an attorney whose experience with a particular matter matches your particular needs, you may be tempted to hire a lawyer described as an expert or specialist in his or her area of law or to hire an attorney who has been in practice for a long time.

Recognize that relevant experience in a particular area of law is far more important than the total number of years that a person has practiced law. It is best to determine the amount of specific experience the attorneys you are considering have had with the type of legal issue you have. Ask them to provide examples of how they have handled similar matters and how many they have handled.

Also make certain that, if your matter will require the attention of more than one attorney at the firm, you ask who else will be working on your matter. It is not uncommon that a more senior attorney will agree to handle a matter and then assign work to less experienced associates. If this is the case, you should ask about the level of experience and expertise of these associates.

Some legal matters will require the attention of a specialist and others will not. You must be the judge on the level of experience your case will require. Fees often vary in accordance with experience and specialized capabilities. Seek a reasonable balance between experience and cost.

FIRM SIZE

Recognize that in most cases it is an individual attorney who will work on a particular file and with whom you will have the most interaction. A sole practitioner or a lawyer practicing in a small group may be able to provide you with personalized attention, whereas a larger firm has many resources to offer. Lawyers at large firms may charge more for their services, however, and you may not want or need to pay extra for a relatively straightforward legal problem. Again, it all depends on your particular needs.

LOCATION

A lawyer's location is another obvious consideration. If many meetings will take place in a city other than your own, it may be advantageous to hire an attorney who lives in your city. Most lawyers charge for the transportation time necessary for them to get to and from meetings and court appearances, so it may be wise to choose someone located near the courthouse or any other location where meetings will take place. You should carefully consider cost and convenience in your selection process.

STEP 3: INTERVIEW THE ATTORNEYS

Once you have narrowed down your list to a few potential candidates, phone each one and seek a personal consultation. It is wise to ask on the phone whether the lawyer charges a fee for the initial consultation. Consulting a lawyer does not obligate you to employ or to retain that lawyer. Most initial consultations are either free of charge or available for a nominal fee, especially if you decide not to employ the consulted attorney. Some attorneys will charge for the initial consultation if they are subsequently hired.

INITIAL CONSULTATION

Do not expect free advice from a lawyer. Top-notch attorneys will welcome opportunities to spend time with potential clients answering questions and being compared with their peers because they know their knowledge and experience will be apparent.

Bring all relevant information and documents as well as a list of questions to the meeting. Be open and honest with the attorney. Do not embellish or hide facts. Providing complete information is essential for the attorney to assess your matter and explain how best to proceed. Except in very limited instances, whatever you tell a lawyer in an interview is confidential and protected by the attorney-client privilege.

It is important to note the distinction between consulting an attorney and retaining that attorney. Only retaining an attorney obligates him or her to act on your behalf. Before leaving a lawyer's office, both of you should be absolutely clear as to whether the lawyer has or has not been hired.

PERSONAL CHEMISTRY

Much of being a good attorney has to do with responsiveness, understanding of a client's particular situation and the ability to communicate. The lawyer who has a bad rapport with a client may not be an effective representative of the client's interests. Because each person is different, the chemistry between a client and an attorney is one of the most important elements of their relationship. Ask many questions and observe closely. Does the lawyer listen to you or interrupt you in the middle of a sentence? Are a variety of options to pursue presented or does the lawyer insist there is only one right way to do everything? Is this someone you want to spend time with? Gut feelings at this stage of the process can tell you much about what it would be like to hire this attorney.

MALPRACTICE INSURANCE

It is important to determine whether the attorney carries malpractice insurance. The financial losses stemming from a poorly handled case can be quite large. If the lawyer does not carry malpractice insurance, it may be impossible to recover any losses if the lawyer commits legal malpractice.

ESTIMATE OF TIME

A lawyer should be able to estimate a timetable for completing a case. This will depend on many variables and asking for a timetable is likely to bring all of these issues into the open. Find out how often the lawyer sends out status reports about a case or matter. A lawyer with little experience may reveal that inexperience if he or she cannot describe the steps necessary to complete a task and estimate how long each will take.

COST

Discuss estimated costs at the initial meeting with an attorney. It is important to know what will and will not be charged and at what rates. Although a lawyer may not be able to give an exact cost, one with experience should be able to provide an estimate of his or her fees.

Do some comparison shopping before hiring your lawyer. Hiring an attorney may require a major outlay of resources so, like any other expenditure, you should find out details such as how often bills are sent out, whether the firm requires a retainer and if there are minimum billing increments. As with any business arrangement, get your agreement in writing.

Lawyers have several different ways that a client may pay the fees for their services:

Flat Fees

The simplest fee payment option is the flat fee. A lawyer charging a flat fee simply quotes a fee for which he or she will do the work. Flat rates were once quite rare; however, recently the flat fee has been growing in popularity. Much of this growth is client-driven and stems from clients' desire to better predict and control the rising cost of legal representation. Today, lawyers are increasingly willing to discuss the possibility of a flat fee for relatively simple legal matters. Bear in mind, however, that low, advertised flat fees may be a ploy to get a potential client in the door in hopes that, once in the office, the client can be convinced that his or her needs are actually far more complex and therefore justify much higher fees.

Hourly Rates

For many matters, a lawyer will charge an hourly rate for time spent on a file. The hourly rate is usually a reflection of the lawyer's competence, experience and overhead expenses. The lowest hourly rate may not be the best deal. An experienced lawyer with higher rates may be able to complete a matter more quickly than a less experienced lawyer with lower rates. A common complaint about hourly rates is that they give the lawyer no incentive to handle a matter in a timely fashion. Before agreeing to hire a lawyer to work for an hourly rate, it is appropriate to request a written estimate of the hours that will be needed, as well as an estimate of how much money will be necessary for miscellaneous expenses.

Retainer Fees

There are two kinds of retainer fees. The first is a variation of the flat fee. Rather than paying a lawyer a flat fee to handle a specific matter, some wealthy individuals or large corporations will pay an attorney a lump sum each year to retain that attorney for the year. In return for this fee, the lawyer agrees to be on call for any legal problems that arise or to manage routine day-to-day legal affairs. The average individual does not have a sufficient volume of legal questions to require this type of setup.

The more common retainer fee is actually just an advance on the hourly rate described above. If it is the first time that a lawyer has represented a particular client or if there is any question about the client's ability to pay, the lawyer may insist upon the payment of a large retainer up front. This money is then placed in a special account and the costs of legal services provided are deducted from that account. A client agreeing to pay this type of retainer is still entitled to periodic written statements detailing how much has been deducted from the account for legal services and, of course, the client is entitled to any money remaining in the account when legal representation has concluded.

Contingent Fees

Another common fee arrangement is the contingent fee. The contingent fee is most common among personal injury attorneys who charge for their services by taking a percentage (the going rate is one-third) of whatever damages are recovered or the amount of money saved for the client, whether through an out-of-court settlement or a jury award. The percentage for which a lawyer asks depends on the difficulty of the issues, the amount of money at stake and the skill and experience of the attorney.

You may be better off with a more experienced attorney because, although the fee may be higher, so may the resulting award.

There are several reasons to be especially careful when hiring a personal injury lawyer to work on a contingent fee basis. Many law firms specializing in these kinds of cases make their money by handling a large number of personal injury cases and settling them quickly. Because of the typical contingent fee arrangement, some lawyers are motivated to recommend accepting early settlement offers made by insurance companies, the usual defendants in such matters. By settling early, both the firm and the client may make less money, but the firm takes its cut of the settlement at a stage when it has incurred few expenses because it has not spent the time and money to fully prepare a case. Be wary of such firms. You have the right to refuse any settlement offer made if the offer does not appear to provide the necessary financial compensation given the nature of the case. These considerations are especially important to consider if you have an injury that will require medical care and medical bills for the rest of your life.

Although contingent fee agreements are quite popular with some attorneys, they are inappropriate in some types of cases, and ethics rules may forbid lawyers from accepting contingent fee arrangements in certain types of matters.

Variable Contingency Fees

Another payment option becoming fairly popular among some lawyers is the variable contingency fee arrangement. In this situation, the attorney's fees vary depending upon when the case is settled. Typical arrangements specify that the attorney collect a specific percentage if the case settles before initiating a formal lawsuit, a larger percentage if the case settles within a year after a lawsuit is filed, and a still larger percentage of any damage award received any time after a year. With this type of arrangement, the lawyer has an incentive not to settle too early because the fee will be greater if a larger settlement can be won by going to trial.

Clarify the exact terms of a contingent fee arrangement before signing it. Almost all contingent fee agreements stipulate that the attorney's expenses are first deducted from any award won, and the remainder of the money is then split on a specified percentage basis. You must make sure, therefore, that you fully understand what kind of costs and fees you will be expected to pay before signing a contingent fee agreement.

Miscellaneous Expenses

Many disputes that clients have with lawyers over money stem from a misunderstanding of the difference between "fees" and "expenses." Regardless of the fee plan a client chooses, most lawyers will charge for their expenses in addition to their fees, regardless of the outcome of the case. Many contingent fee clients, lured by attorneys claiming, "no fees unless we recover for you," have been shocked to find out, after failing to recover any money on their claims, that they owe money to their lawyers. The client may indeed pay no fees unless the case is successful but may still be responsible for sizable expenses incurred handling the case, regardless of its outcome. Many law firms bill incidentals, such as photocopying and postage, at rates far higher than what those services would cost at an independent copy center or post office, so it is important to discuss specific details.

BENEFITS OF THE PROCESS

The three-step process described above should begin with a list of names and, after diligent research and meetings, conclude with one name standing out above the others as the best choice. This *Guide* provides a valuable resource and starting point for your selection process by providing a list of Leading Minnesota Attorneys and information about the nature of their practice and experience.

ABBREVIATION KEY

The attorneys whose biographical profiles appear in this book were chosen by their peers as the most respected legal counsel in Minnesota.

Use these profiles as a resource of attorneys who can best assist you with your legal needs. The "Extensive Experience" points will assist you as a quick reference, but be certain to read the profiles thoroughly to gain the most complete understanding of each attorney's capabilities.

Remember, the hiring of an attorney is an important decision that should not be based solely on marketing materials and advertisements. Before deciding, ask the attorneys you are considering for free written information about their qualifications and experience. Refer to the chapter of this *Guide,* "How to Select an Attorney," for a description of a sound process to use in evaluating attorneys and selecting the correct one for your needs.

App.	Appellate
Cir.	Circuit
Ct.	Court
Dist.	District
Sup.	Supreme
JD	Juris Doctorate (Doctor of Law)
LL	Law Degree
LLB	Legum Baccalaureus (Bachelor of Laws)
LLD	Legum Doctor (Doctor of Laws)
LLM	Legum Magister (Master of Laws)
ADR	Alternative Dispute Resolution
ABA	American Bar Association
ATLA	Association of Trial Lawyers of America
ABOTA	American Board of Trial Advocates
NACDL	National Association of Criminal Defense Lawyers
HCBA	Hennepin County Bar Association
MSBA	Minnesota State Bar Association
MTLA	Minnesota Trial Lawyers Association
RCBA	Ramsey County Bar Association
NBTA	National Board of Trial Advocacy

ARTS, ENTERTAINMENT & SPORTS LAW

The Sports Law section was written by John Wendt at the University of St. Thomas.

The law of arts, entertainment and media crosses over many lines. A person involved in one of these areas may be confronted with issues on contracts, copyright, trademarks, constitutional rights, business organization and tax. This chapter will highlight some of the specific issues a person may encounter in the areas of art, entertainment or media law.

PROTECTING CREATIVE WORK

It is essential for artists to protect their rights in their creation. The law provides artists rights when creating an original work. These rights are exclusive to the creator; however, the creator may grant licenses to the work. Although the law grants the creator rights, it is up to him or her to protect and enforce those rights.

COPYRIGHT INFRINGEMENT

When a party uses a copyrighted work without authorization and the use violates one of the artist's exclusive rights, infringement occurs. The copyright owner can bring a federal civil action against the infringer. The plaintiff in an infringement action must prove that he or she is the copyright owner and that the defendant infringed upon one of the plaintiff's exclusive rights. Copyright registration presumes that the person registered as the owner is the copyright owner. The plaintiff has the burden of proving that the defendant had access to the plaintiff's work and the defendant's work is substantially similar to the plaintiff's. Once the plaintiff proves these two elements, the burden shifts to the defendant to prove that his or her work was created independently. Before the infringement issue is resolved through a trial or settlement, a copyright owner can go to court and ask for a restraining order against the defendant to prevent him or her from continuing the alleged infringement activity. If the court determines the activity to be infringement, it may grant an injunction, permanently barring the defendant's actions. A plaintiff who prevails in an infringement case can recover money damages as provided by statute or actual damages incurred as a result of the infringement, plus any profits made by the infringer–the choice is the plaintiff's. The court may also grant attorney's fees in a successful infringement case. A defense to an infringement claim is that one is an innocent infringer. This is a person who relies on an authorized copy where the copyright notice has been omitted and he or she had no other reason to believe the work was protected. An innocent infringer is not liable for actual or statutory damages.

TRADEMARK REGISTRATION OF NAMES

A trademark is a word, symbol, design, or a combination that identifies a party's goods and services and distinguishes them from another's goods and services. Artists and entertainers provide goods like paintings, compact discs, photographs and poems, and provide services in live performances. An artist's or entertainer's name can sell merchandise and tickets. The name used by an artist or entertainer can be a trademark or service mark. Because an artist's or entertainer's creativity and work have gone into producing his or her goods and services, it may be prudent to protect his or her name by trademark or service mark registration. As in copyright infringement, a party who believes her trademark has been infringed may bring a private, civil action for money damages and/or injunctive relief.

Artists and entertainers who are not incorporated and are doing business under a name other than their own are required to file that name with the Minnesota Secretary of State's office.

LICENSES

A person may derive income from reproducing, distributing, performing or displaying a copyrighted work, or by creating additional works based upon a copyrighted work. Either the artist or a party who buys the rights from the artist to do any or all of those activities can generate this income. The buyer of rights in a work has a license. This license may be exclusive or nonexclusive. The artist or entertainer may receive a flat fee or a percentage of the profits for the license. It is important to receive legal representation before a person relinquishes rights and grants a license to a creation.

ARTISTS' MORAL RIGHTS

It is believed that there is a unique bond between an artist and the work he or she creates. Based on this belief, there are specific rights for artists. These rights are known as moral rights (*droit moral*). Moral rights protect, among other things, the integrity of an artist's work so that it cannot be changed without his or her permission. Copyright protection is part of artists' moral rights.

Moral rights originated in France and are recognized in a number of countries including, in a limited way, the United States. However, the United States does not recognize all moral rights. There are also differences between states in protecting artists' moral rights. If an artist wants certain rights that are not provided by law, one option is to put these rights into a contract. The following are some of the moral rights.

RIGHT TO CREATE

The right of an artist to create or not create a work is included in moral rights. Disputes over the right to create usually arise when an artist refuses to create or complete a work for which he or she was commissioned. Artists are rarely forced to create because courts are reluctant to force someone to perform services. The party contracting for the work may also be reluctant to have the artist forced to finish the work. However, an artist who fails to fulfill his or her duties under a contract is liable for damages.

NAME ATTRIBUTION

In 1990, the federal Visual Artists Rights Act (VARA) was passed. This act applies to paintings, drawings, prints or sculptures, and amends the Copyright Law by providing certain artists with attribution and integrity rights. VARA permits an artist to claim credit for the work he or she has created. The artist also has the right to stop the use of his or her name as the artist of a work if the work is distorted, mutilated or modified, and credit to such work would be prejudicial to the artist's honor or reputation.

INTEGRITY

VARA provides artists the right to prevent any intentional distortion, mutilation or other modification of work that would be prejudicial to the artist's honor or reputation. VARA also provides the artist the right to prevent destruction of a work of recognized stature. Scholars, curators and collectors determine what constitutes a work of recognized stature. This protection may be limited if the work is placed on a building.

ARTISTS' ECONOMIC RIGHTS

Artists' economic rights give an artist the right to participate in the profits from resales of his or her work. Authors and entertainers typically enjoy royalty payments from subsequent reproduction and syndication. Fine artists, on the other hand, receive payment upon the initial sale only and unfortunately fail to receive profits from their work's resale. The United States and Minnesota do not provide economic rights to artists. If an artist includes in a sales contract a provision requiring a share of profits from any resale, enforcement of such a provision may be a problem.

INDEPENDENT CONTRACTOR OR EMPLOYEE

It is essential that an artist or entertainer who is hired to create a work determines whether he or she is an independent contractor or an employee. Copyright does not vest in an employee creating a work, but it does vest in an independent contractor hired to create a work. An employee creating work for her employer has created a "work for hire" and the copyright belongs to the employer. A person who has been hired to create work for another and is not an employee retains the copyright unless there is a written relinquishment of these rights.

TAXATION

The method of income taxation depends on whether a person is an employee or an independent contractor. Employers withhold and pay taxes for employees, while independent contractors are responsible for paying their own taxes. There are a few other tax issues on which an artist or entertainer may wish to consult a qualified attorney. If an artist or entertainer is conducting a business, expenses related to this business may be deducted from his or her income and result in paying fewer taxes. A person should make sure he or she is applying for deductions to their fullest benefit. Also, because the income of artists and entertainers can be sporadic and result in years of low income and other years of higher income, a person may want to determine if there is a way that the income could be staggered to pay a lower tax rate and defer the payment of taxes. Finally, artists may wish to make charitable contributions of work and take a deduction on their tax return. Unfortunately, the Internal Revenue Service only allows artists to deduct the costs of the materials and supplies used and not the value of time, services or the fair market value of the work.

CONSIGNMENT

Minnesota statutes state that when an artist delivers a work of art to an art dealer for exhibition or sale on a compensation basis, the art dealer's acceptance of the work constitutes a consignment unless there is an outright sale. A consignment of art means the art dealer is an agent of the artist for the purpose of sale or exhibition, the art dealer holds the art in trust and it is not subject to the art dealer's creditors, the art dealer is responsible for any damage or loss of art while it is in his or her possession, and proceeds from the art's sale must be held in trust for the artist's benefit.

ENTERTAINMENT AGENCIES

Minnesota statutes require that any person involved in procuring, offering or promising employment or engagements for three or more artists or groups of artists at any one time, or who has a written contract or a verbal agreement with an establishment or an individual to provide artists for one or more engagements, must be licensed as an entertainment agency by the Minnesota Department of Labor and

Industry. Entertainment agencies are also required to submit to the Department of Labor and Industry the forms of contracts they will use and a schedule of fees to be charged and collected.

CONTRACTS

It is essential that when an artist or entertainer contemplates relinquishing rights or signing a long-term performance contract, he or she receive legal counsel, as contracts such as these can be complex and have far-reaching effects. Also, it almost goes without saying that artists and entertainers should be cautious about the people with whom they enter into contracts. Although one may have a binding legal agreement, if it is with an unscrupulous person, enforcing such a contract may be very difficult.

OBSCENITY

Although the United States Constitution guarantees one the freedom of expression, this right has limitations—one of which is obscenity. Obscene material is not entitled to constitutional protection. The United States Supreme Court created the following test to use in determining whether material is obscene or not: whether the average person applying contemporary community standards would find that the work, taken as a whole, appeals to the prurient interest; whether the works depict or describe, in a patently offensive way, sexual conduct specifically defined by the applicable state law; and whether the work, taken as a whole, lacks serious literary, artistic, political or scientific value. This standard is difficult to apply in the abstract, and can vary widely from community to community.

DEFAMATION

The down side of free speech, however, is that injudicious speech can sometimes lead to a defamation suit. Defamation is a false statement that damages another person's reputation or character. Statements that falsely accuse one of a crime, dishonesty in business, or unchastity will probably be found defamatory. Libel is written defamation and slander is spoken defamation. There have been many defamation cases, and the requirements for proving a defamation case are many and varied depending on who the plaintiff is and what was said or written. This section will outline the basic components of a defamation case and the possible defenses. It should be noted that an estate of a dead person cannot bring an action for defamation.

A defamatory statement must be included in a statement of fact, not a statement of opinion, to be actionable. There is a difference between stating a person is "a jerk" (opinion) and a person is "a convicted murderer" (fact). Statements are defamatory if they injure a person's reputation, or expose him or her to contempt, ridicule, degradation or hatred. The statement must also be false. No matter how damaging a statement, if it is true, there is no action for defamation, although there may be grounds for a slightly different lawsuit, such as harassment. In order to bring an action for defamation, the statement must be communicated to a third party; this is called publication. The statement must also identify the party being defamed. A person need not be identified by name, but a reasonable person must be able to identify the plaintiff from the statement.

Once a plaintiff in a defamation case has proven that the defendant published a false, defamatory statement of fact about the plaintiff, the plaintiff must prove that the statement was published with either actual malice or negligence. The standard used depends on whether the plaintiff is considered a public figure or a private person. A public figure can be a celebrity, politician, police officer, or citizen active in public policy. If the plaintiff is held to be a public figure, he or she must prove that the defendant acted maliciously by deliberately failing to verify the statements. A plaintiff who is a private person must prove that the defendant was negligent in publishing the statement and should have known that the statement was false.

As mentioned before, truth is a defense to a defamation action. Also, proof that a statement was an opinion or that the statement was made during a judicial or legislative proceeding, or made by a government official while conducting business, are defenses.

SPORTS LAW

David Stern, National Basketball Association commissioner, is a lawyer. Gary Bettman, National Hockey League commissioner, is a lawyer, too. Anita De Frantz, the first woman International Olympic Committee vice president, is an attorney, and so is famous sports agent Leigh Steinberg. These are just some of the people involved in sports law. This section will examine the various areas of sports law.

DEFINITION

Sports law runs with entertainment law; in fact, at times the two are blended. Hard at times to define, sports law's existence lies in terms of differentiation. Some legal doctrines, such as baseball's antitrust exemptions, are unique to sports. In other cases, the legal doctrine may not be unique, but the factual situation will set it apart. For example, Title IX and gender equity are based on the same concepts as statutes designed to eliminate discrimination in housing, education and employment, but considered in the light of intercollegiate athletics, especially in revenue generating sports, the practical rules may be different. On top of this is an additional layer the role that sports plays in society. As much as society downplays the value of sports, in reality we value it highly. How many newspapers have a separate sports section? How many television stations have a special segment dealing just with sports? What market share of the television audience does the NCAA Basketball Final Four or the Olympics have? In this light, suddenly sports do not seem so trivial.

WHAT ARE SOME OF THE DIFFERENT ROLES IN THE SPORTS INDUSTRY?

PROFESSIONAL SPORTS

When one thinks of a sports lawyer, one immediately thinks of an agent—someone who represents a professional athlete or a "stable" of professional athletes. But an attorney who practices sports law will see a wide variety of issues and should be cautioned to be careful not to pursue this one area of sports law alone—representation is just one segment. Sports law includes financing for stadiums, television rights, sponsorship agreements, labor management negotiations and governmental relationships. A recent example of stadium licensing and sponsorship is the MCI Center, which will earn about $60 million in sign revenue this year. US Airways, Coca Cola, Chevy Chase Bank, and Washington Gas all signed multiyear charter sponsorships with the MCI Center at $5 million a year per company (this is in addition to MCI's $44 million naming rights agreement. Also, the Washington Redskins recently hired ProServe to sell stadium ads at the new Jack Kent Cooke Stadium. Budweiser, Sprint, NationsBank and Coca-Cola each bought 24' x 32' signs behind each end zone that could cost as much as $350,000 to $500,000 per year. Signage is everywhere, including the field tunnel signs that will cost $125,000. For $15,000, one can purchase a 30-second commercial on the Jumbotron.

Other legal issues in professional sports include partnerships, such as the new deal between the CBA and New Line TV designed to build the CBA into a national brand through licensing, TV and sponsorship opportunities. Partnership has even extended to Nike's altering of the Green Bay Packers' uniforms by designing the sleeves with three stripes instead of the five previously worn. There are financing and construction issues, especially with the recent rash of team moves and threatened moves if new stadiums aren't built. Finally, with the major realignment discussions within Major League Baseball, San Francisco Giants Owner Peter M. Magowan may take his fellow owners to court. Magowan wants to block the plan, which would move the Oakland Athletics to the National League, on the basis that the Giants franchise agreement decrees that the Bay Area is "Giants territory."

ATHLETE REPRESENTATION

If an agent represents an athlete, what does the job involve? Negotiating his or her contract? Investing his or her money? Who is a sports agent? Originally, athletes represented themselves in contract negotiations—agents were not even allowed in the building. The pendulum seems to have swung the other way, with some agents themselves becoming superstars. An attorney seeking to practice solely in athlete representation faces difficult challenges. The time and monetary costs of running such a practice are extremely high, and the professional client pool is limited. In addition, sports agents do not have to be attorneys. Agents have been everything from former players to dentists. Because the competition for clients is so keen, often the pursuit is unprincipled. Given the ethical restrictions all attorneys face, it is very difficult to compete. Finally, there are also large firms, like JMG and ProServe, that combine legal, marketing and sometimes investment services, among others. As a result, others who practice sports or sports and entertainment law do so along with another part of their practices. What do sports attorneys/agents do? If they are involved in representation, their basic role is the same as their basic role as an attorney: to advise, counsel and represent their clients throughout their careers. 'Career' might be from the initial negotiating to termination. An agent's services may range from basic contract negotiation to a complete personal and financial management package, including endorsements. Many agents sell themselves to potential clients as being able to get something more than anyone else. However, with the NFL, NBA or Major League Baseball, a great deal of the player's contract is predetermined by his or her respective collective bargaining agreement. The one area that has seen tremendous growth is endorsements. Sports personalities have been able to greatly increase their earnings off the field through product endorsements. Michael Jordan and Tiger Woods have created economic empires. Joe Namath recently cashed in on his fame in a commercial in which he makes a comeback just for the chance to play in Nike's new football cleats and trainers. And even the Vermont Teddy Bear Company signed Green Bay Packer Mark Chmura as a spokesperson for its line of NFL-licensed products.

NCAA AND COLLEGE ATHLETICS

Intercollegiate athletics' issues range from compliance to corporate sponsorship. Perhaps no field has experienced the growth explosion that NCAA compliance has. Even in this area, with millions of dollars invested and the success of their intercollegiate athletic programs at stake, programs have literally spent millions not only in defense of NCAA charges but also in compliance. Additionally, there has been a shift in compliance to a "come forward" approach when dealing with an NCAA allegation. If an institution believes that an infraction has occurred, it immediately begins an investigation and informs the NCAA. Like the philosophy permeating environmental law, schools are spending a great deal of resources on education and proactiveness. Initially, this focus was strictly on NCAA Division I schools, especially when dealing with revenue-producing sports like football and basketball. But compliance even extends to recruiting violations in such sports as synchronized swimming, and it extends to NCAA Division II and III schools. This year, Title IX is celebrating its 25th anniversary. Before 1972, approximately 300,000 girls and women participated in sports; today their numbers total 2.37 million. Yet there are claims that male athletes have almost twice as many opportunities to play in school and college athletic programs and over $184,000 more in athletic scholarships than their female counterparts. In June 1997, the National Women's Law Center filed 25 separate sexual discrimination complaints against universities with the Department of Education Office of Civil Rights. Finally, intercollegiate athletics' marketing and licensing is growing. Fans want to be identified with athletic programs, and the demand for merchandise with the college trademark is growing at a phenomenal rate. Licensing programs have been instituted in nearly every major university. Some questions that schools may face include: Should the University have its own licensing program or use a licensing agent? What marks will be registered? What collateral marks and products will be sold?

AMATEUR SPORTS

Perhaps no other area of sports has seen such a fundamental change than amateur sports. The Amateur Sports Act of 1978 established a new framework for amateur sports in the United States. After years of haggling between the United States Olympic Committee, the Amateur Athletic Union, NCAA and other sports organizations, Congress finally stepped in. Under the Amateur Sports Act, the United States Olympic Committee elects one national governing body for each Olympic or Pan-American sport. Examples include United States Gymnastics, the United States Figure Skating Association and USA Basketball. Under the act, national governing bodies can define what is an "amateur" athlete and determine eligibility. Historically, many amateurs were college athletes and not being paid for their services. Many Americans remember the 1980 United States hockey team's "Miracle on Ice" victory over the "professionals" from the former Soviet Union. However, with the rise of Juan Antonio Samaranch, the philosophy of international competition has changed to 'the best shall compete and it shall be fair.' This philosophy made the United States basketball "Dream Team" and professionals competing in hockey, tennis and figure skating possible. There are many issues facing national governing bodies; for example, United States Swimming, which does not get a great deal of publicity when compared to figure skating, more than 350,000 members—the majority of whom are minors. The legal issue spectrum confronting United States Swimming range from tort liability and accidents to nonprofit incorporation issues and corporate sponsorship. Finally, as an outgrowth of, among others, the Tonya Harding and Butch Reynolds situations, the International Olympic Committee and the United States Olympic Committee have each come up with a new method of dispute resolution. Once an athlete joins a national governing body, he or she and the national governing body agree to be bound by the dispute resolution system. If a dispute arises between an athlete and a national governing body on a topic such as eligibility, drug violations, etc., an American Arbitration Association special panel hears the dispute. The new International Court of Arbitration for Sport handles international disputes. Approximately 140 arbitrators from 35 countries will convene, hear the dispute and render a decision on the sport. Cases range from invalid termination of a broadcasting rights contract to horse doping. In addition, President Samaranch recently indicated that commercial disputes arising at the Games of the XXVII Olympiad in Sidney, Australia, will be also settled by the CAS.

CONCLUSION

The field is wide and varied, but it is often hard to get started if you think that the only opportunities lie in athlete representation. Sports law is a broad legal discipline that needs individuals who can combine their vocation and avocation in a love for sports law.

ARTS, ENTERTAINMENT & SPORTS LAW

Abdo & Abdo, P.A.
710 Northstar West
625 Marquette Avenue
Minneapolis, MN 55402
Phone: (612) 333-1526
Fax: (612) 342-2608

KENNETH J. ABDO

KENNETH J. ABDO: A former professional musician and disc jockey, Mr. Abdo is an attorney, a principal shareholder and Vice President of Abdo & Abdo, P.A. He concentrates in business, entertainment, intellectual property, employment and contract law, and negotiates and counsels on a wide range of entertainment contracts and matters. Mr. Abdo is an adjunct professor of art, entertainment and sports law at William Mitchell and Hamline University Law Schools, where he lectures on music, film, media, sports, trademarks and copyrights. He also lectures and writes for various legal and public audiences. His writing includes two chapters in *The Practical Musician,* 1993.
Education: JD 1982, William Mitchell (staff writer, *William Mitchell Law Review;* Moot Court Society); BA 1979, University of Minnesota (Phi Beta Kappa; Omicron Delta Kappa).
Admitted: 1983 Minnesota; 1983 U.S. Dist. Ct. (MN).
Employment History: Law Clerk/Attorney 1979-present, Abdo & Abdo, P.A.
Representative Clients: Mr. Abdo's clients include businesses and individuals in the entertainment business, including radio and television talents and stations, actors, for-profit and nonprofit theaters, music recording studios, independent film and music projects, comedians, agents, managers, writers, musicians, film and theater production companies, special event production companies, literary publishers, sports figures, entertainer licensers and merchandisers.
Professional Associations: ABA [Forum on Entertainment and Sports Industry annual conference (Planning Committee)]; MSBA [Arts and Entertainment Law Section (Chair 1991-93)]; Music Law Committee (Chair 1993-present); Seminar on Entertainment and Sports Law (Cochair 1992-present).
Community Involvement: The Cricket Theatre [Board of Directors (Chair)]; Concerts for the Environment; Midwest Center for Arts, Entertainment and Law (Board of Directors); Minneapolis Athletic Club (Board of Directors); Youth Forum Minnesota (Board of Directors).
Firm: Since 1936, Abdo & Abdo, P.A., has provided businesses and individuals with personalized legal services. The firm's six attorneys provide legal counsel focused on small and medium-sized businesses' specific needs, including start-ups, maintenance, mergers, acquisitions, partnerships, securities, real estate, employment, intellectual property (copyrights and trademarks), entertainment, debtor, creditor, and general and complex litigation. The firm also serves the legal needs of individuals, professionals and business owners in employment law, contracts, wills, probate and estate planning. *See complete firm profile in the Firm Profiles section.*

ARTS, ENTERTAINMENT & SPORTS LAW

Patterson & Keough, P.A.
1200 Rand Tower
527 Marquette Avenue South
Minneapolis, MN 55402

Phone: (612) 349-5767
Fax: (612) 349-9266
800: (800) 331-4537
E-mail: ljd@pklaw.com

**LAURA J.
DANIELSON**

LAURA J. DANIELSON: Ms. Danielson represents clients in immigration and arts and entertainment matters with special emphasis on arts and business-related immigration. She represents foreign artists, entertainers, athletes, engineers, scientists, medical personnel and other professionals in nonimmigrant and immigrant visa matters. Ms. Danielson also handles family immigration, asylum, copyright, license and contract cases for individual artists and arts organizations. She teaches immigration law at the University of Minnesota and has taught arts and entertainment law at William Mitchell and Hamline Law Schools. She also lectures nationally and locally on arts related immigration issues. She is a former legal writing instructor at William Mitchell and the University of Minnesota Law Schools, has written numerous nationally published articles and was a consulting editor for *The Practical Musician.*

Education: JD 1989 cum laude, University of Minnesota; BA 1977, Carleton College.
Admitted: 1989 Minnesota; 1994 U.S. Dist. Ct. (MN).
Employment History: Attorney/Officer 1994-present, Patterson & Keough, P.A.; Partner 1991-1994, Danielson & Begley, P.A.; Attorney 1989-91, John M. Roth & Associates.
Representative Clients: Ms. Danielson represents numerous businesses, arts organizations and individuals.
Professional Associations: Minnesota Advocates for Human Rights (Board Member 1995-present); MSBA [Arts and Entertainment Section (Treasurer; Vice Chair 1991-93)]; American Immigration Lawyers Assn. 1989-present.
Community Involvement: Southern Theatre (Board Member 1991-present).
Firm: Patterson & Keough, P.A., provides services in intellectual property, representing clients in the areas of copyrights, trademarks, patents, trade secrets, related litigation, licensing and immigration. The firm serves a broad spectrum of clients ranging from creative individuals to Fortune 500 companies. Since its inception in 1991, Patterson & Keough, P.A.'s practice has focused on meeting the needs of a full range of intellectual property clients—from inventors and engineers to artists and entertainers.

Extensive Experience In:
- Arts Immigration
- Nonprofits
- Fine Arts

ARTS, ENTERTAINMENT & SPORTS LAW

Barbara J. Gislason & Associates
506 St. Anthony Main
219 SE Main Street
Minneapolis, MN 55414

Phone: (612) 331-8033
Fax: (612) 331-8115
E-mail: bjgislason@aol.com

BARBARA J.
GISLASON

BARBARA J. GISLASON: A third-generation attorney, Ms. Gislason served as the founding chair of the Minnesota State Bar Association's Art & Entertainment Law Section. In addition to being a highly skilled contract negotiator, Ms. Gislason has gained a reputation as a dynamic and respected litigator. She is a guest lecturer at educational institutions and conferences throughout the United States. As a sign of the times, she has developed alternative dispute resolution skills and serves on the Minnesota Supreme Court roster as a qualified Mediator and Arbitrator.
Education: JD 1980, William Mitchell; BA 1974, Carleton College.
Admitted: 1980 Minnesota; 1980 U.S. Dist. Ct. (MN); 1983 U.S. Ct. App. (8th Cir.); 1988 U.S. Sup. Ct.
Employment History: 1995-present, Gislason Mediation and Arbitration Services; 1992-present, The Gislason Agency (literary agency); 1985-present, Barbara J. Gislason & Associates, Attorneys at Law; Panel Arbitrator/Referee 1987-present, Hennepin County District Court; Adjunct Professor 1985-90, Minneapolis College of Art and Design; Adjunct Professor 1983-84, Hamline University School of Law; Associate 1980-85, Babcock, Locher, Neilson & Mannella.
Representative Clients: Ms. Gislason, though best known for her expertise in literary publishing and the visual arts, represents a broad spectrum of art and entertainment clients, including educational developers, media personalities, galleries, small presses, musicians, fashion designers, photographers, software developers, fine artists and playwrights. In addition, as a literary agent, Ms. Gislason represents nationally acclaimed authors.
Professional Associations: MSBA [Internet Committee; Computer Law Section (International Committee Chair 1991-92); Art & Entertainment Law Section (Chair 1990-91); Art Law Committee (Chair 1989-90); Bar-Media Committee (Symposium Chair 1987-88); Computer Law Section (Litigation Committee Chair 1987-88)]; Minnesota Intellectual Property Law Assn. [Copyright Committee (Chair 1989-91)].
Community Involvement: Minnesota State Board of Law Examiners (Advisory Panel 1989-93); Alexandra House for battered women (Legal Panel 1984-93); Minnesota State Arts Board (Advisory Panel 1990-91); MSBA [Law Day Committee (Chair 1984)].
Firm: Barbara J. Gislason & Associates, founded in 1985, and Gislason Mediation and Arbitration Services, founded in 1995, provide commendable, cost-effective services for their clients. The Gislason Agency represents fiction and nonfiction writers. In addition to her Minneapolis office, Ms. Gislason has a satellite office at 7400 University Avenue NE, Fridley, MN 55432. Phone: (612) 572-9297, Fax (612) 571-1936.

Extensive Experience In:
• Complex Publishing Issues
• A Skilled Navigator
• Gislason, Attorney & Agent

ARTS, ENTERTAINMENT & SPORTS LAW

Abdo & Abdo, P.A.
710 Northstar West
625 Marquette Avenue
Minneapolis, MN 55402

Phone: (612) 333-1526
Fax: (612) 342-2608

DANIEL M.
SATORIUS

DANIEL M. SATORIUS: Mr. Satorius' practice includes assisting individuals and businesses in the development of various forms of intellectual property within and outside the entertainment industry. His experience as a professional musician and award-winning film maker provides him with practical understanding and knowledge of the entertainment industry. He has taught numerous courses as an adjunct professor on the legal and business aspects of film and television production at William Mitchell College of Law, Film in the Cities, Inver Hill Community College, Minneapolis Community College, and Music Tech. Mr Satorius frequently writes and lectures on topics relating to intellectual property and the entertainment industries.

Education: JD 1978, Southern Illinois University; MA 1975, University of Iowa; BA 1973, University of Iowa.

Admitted: 1979 Minnesota; 1978 Illinois; 1980 U.S. Dist. Ct. (MN).

Representative Clients: Mr. Satorius represents producers, publishers, distributors, artists, writers and performers in the music, motion picture, television, book publishing, computer and interactive media industries.

Professional Associations: MSBA [Arts and Entertainment Law Section (Chair); Music Law Committee (Chair)]; ABA (Forum on the Entertainment and Sports Industries).

Community Involvement: Independent Feature Project/North; Minnesota Blockbuster McKnight Film Fund; Screenwriters Workshop; Resources in Counseling for the Arts; Governor's Task Force on Music and Recording Arts Industry in Minnesota (Education Subcommittee; Industrial Development Subcommittee).

Firm: Since 1936, Abdo & Abdo, P.A , has provided businesses and individuals with personalized legal services. The firm's six attorneys provide legal counsel focused on small and medium-sized businesses' specific needs, including start-ups, maintenance, mergers, acquisitions, partnerships, securities, real estate, employment, intellectual property (copyrights and trademarks), entertainment, debtor, creditor, and general and complex litigation. The firm also serves the legal needs of individuals, professionals and business owners in employment law, contracts, wills, probate and estate planning. *See complete firm profile in the Firm Profiles section.*

Extensive Experience In:
• Entertainment Issues
• Copyright
• Trademark

ABDO & ABDO, P.A.

710 Northstar West - 625 Marquette Avenue - Minneapolis, MN 55402
Phone: (612) 333-1526, Fax: (612) 342-2608

Abdo & Abdo, P.A., has provided personalized legal services for businesses and individuals since 1936. The firm provides legal counsel focused on the specific needs of small- and medium-sized businesses. It addresses a wide spectrum of corporate and business practice areas, including start-ups, maintenance, mergers, acquisitions, securities, real estate, employment, intellectual property (copyrights and trademarks), entertainment, debtor, creditor, general and complex litigation. The firm further serves the legal needs of individuals, professionals and business owners in employment, contract, wills, probate, estate planning and preparation of various agreements. Abdo & Abdo, P.A., offers the advantage of attorneys who have a broad and practical understanding of legal issues affecting businesses and individuals. The firm's goal is personal, effective representation for a reasonable fee.

Kenneth J. Abdo has helped build the firm into one of the Midwest's most visible and active entertainment law practices. He is a contributing author to *The Practical Musician,* a legal guidebook for musicians. His areas of concentration include entertainment (music, film, television, theater, literary publishing and broadcast media talent contracts), employment contracts, corporate, general business, intellectual property and general contract law.

Robert P. Abdo is a recognized leader in business law and in the community. He is a long-time member of the securities, corporate and real estate sections of the Hennepin County Bar Association. Mr. Abdo concentrates on securities, real estate, wills, estate and general business and corporate law matters, including mergers and acquisitions, contracts and film, television and other entertainment financing.

Keith J. Broady is known as an expert practitioner in complex civil and litigation matters. He serves as an arbitrator for civil cases for the Hennepin County District Court and as an arbitrator for the Hennepin County Bar Association's Legal Fee Arbitration Committee. He is also listed as an arbitrator and mediator on the neutral roster for the Minnesota State Court system. He focuses on civil litigation, commercial law, real estate and probate.

Steven R. Hedges practices in civil litigation, corporate, employment and administrative law. In civil trial work, he has headed litigation teams in complex cases involving multi-state contract litigation against a major transportation company (in which he obtained a multimillion dollar judgment), corporate securities disputes, sexual harassment claims and government whistleblower liability.

Timothy C. Matson brings a broad understanding of intellectual property and excellent research skills to the firm. He practices in corporate, entertainment, litigation and intellectual property law. He has authored articles on entertainment and First Amendment issues for the Minnesota State Bar Association's Arts & Entertainment Law Section and the Minnesota Music Academy. He is a member of the MSBA's Sports Law Committee.

Daniel M. Satorius has been an important figure in the development of Minnesota's film and music industries. He was chair of the Minnesota State Bar Association's Arts & Entertainment Law Section and chair of its Music Law Committee. His representation includes assisting individuals and businesses in the development of various forms of intellectual property within and outside the entertainment industry.

BANKRUPTCY LAW:
INDIVIDUAL

If a person falls behind in paying off debts and it appears that he or she will not be able to make payments as they come due, it is better to take action rather than let one's financial situation deteriorate. For many people, the answer to financial problems is to declare bankruptcy, a legal proceeding in federal court that allows a person to be released from the obligation of paying some or all of his or her debts.

It is often said that bankruptcy gives a debtor a fresh start, but filing bankruptcy is not a panacea for all financial problems because it is not painless. Declaring bankruptcy can seriously damage a person's credit rating, making it difficult to establish credit or take out loans. Many people can work themselves out of even very serious debt without ever going near a bankruptcy court, so declaring bankruptcy should not be an automatic first step for someone experiencing financial problems.

THE BANKRUPTCY CODE

Bankruptcy law is federal law. The United States Constitution grants to the federal government the exclusive right to make bankruptcy laws. Pursuant to this authority, the federal government created the Bankruptcy Code, Bankruptcy Rules of Procedure, and a system of Bankruptcy courts to handle bankruptcies throughout the country. This is not to say that bankruptcy law is uniform throughout the nation, however. Although the federal government has final authority to make all bankruptcy laws, in some instances the Bankruptcy Code grants to individual states the power to deviate from federal rules in limited circumstances. For instance, the bankruptcy code allows a debtor to keep certain assets, known as exempt assets, that creditors cannot reach to satisfy a debt. The bankruptcy code gives states the authority to expand the categories of exempt assets if they choose. Thus, the amount of assets beyond the reach of creditors differs depending upon the state where the debtor files for bankruptcy.

The Bankruptcy Code creates different categories of bankruptcy, known as chapters, appropriate for different debtors. The two most common forms of consumer bankruptcy are Chapter 7 and Chapter 13.

CHAPTER 7

The vast majority of bankruptcy cases are Chapter 7 cases. Chapter 7 is often called liquidation bankruptcy. Chapter 7 is commonly used by individuals who want to walk away from their debt simply, but it may also be used by businesses that want to terminate their operations and liquidate their assets. When a debtor files Chapter 7, the bankruptcy court appoints a person—the trustee—to administer the case. The debtor turns over some or all of his or her debts and assets to the trustee. The trustee then liquidates the property by selling it off and dividing the resulting cash among the creditors.

STEP 1: PETITION AND SCHEDULES

A Chapter 7 case begins when the debtor files a petition with the bankruptcy court. Any individual, partnership, or corporation can file Chapter 7 regardless of the amount of debt or whether the debtor is solvent or insolvent. The petition should be filed with the court serving the area where the debtor lives or where his or her principal place of business or assets are located.

Along with the petition, or shortly thereafter, the debtor files with the court several schedules listing current income and expenditures, a statement of financial affairs, all executor contracts, existing or potential lawsuits by or against the debtor and any recent transfers of assets. If a debtor does not reveal a debt in these schedules, the bankruptcy court cannot discharge or cancel that debt. Any debt omitted from these schedules is called a nonscheduled debt and is not affected by the bankruptcy.

STEP 2: STAY

Filing the petition automatically stops (stays) all of the listed creditors from trying to collect the money they are owed. The stay arises automatically, without any judicial action, although the court usually does notify creditors of the filing of the petition. The stay is effective from the time of filing, even if the creditors do not receive notice until much later. As long as the stay is in effect, creditors cannot generally start or continue actions against the debtor to collect on the debt. Lawsuits, garnishment actions and even telephone calls to the debtor must cease.

STEP 3: CREDITORS MEETING

After the debtor files a Chapter 7 petition, the court appoints a trustee to administer the case and liquidate assets. The trustee usually calls a meeting of the debtor, the debtor's attorney and the creditors. The debtor must attend this meeting; creditors may attend in order to ask questions and examine documents concerning the debtor's financial affairs and property. In most consumer bankruptcies, all of the debtor's assets are either exempt or subject to valid liens, so there are no assets for creditors to pursue. In these cases, known as "no asset" cases, it is likely that no creditors show up at the creditors meeting. If it appears that a case will have assets to pursue, creditors usually show up at this meeting to gather information about the case because they plan to ask the bankruptcy judge to declare some of the debts nondischargeable, they plan to challenge the exempt status of some asset, or they plan to file claims.

STEP 4: CLAIMS

After the creditors meeting, the creditors can file a claim against the debtor with the court. If the case has nonexempt assets free of security interests, these will be used to satisfy valid claims.

STEP 5: LIQUIDATION, DISCHARGE AND REAFFIRMATION

The trustee's primary role is to sell off the debtor's nonexempt assets in a way that maximizes the amount the creditors receive for their claims. Revenues from assets subject to security interests, such as property subject to a mortgage, is used to satisfy the debt on the particular asset. A Chapter 7 bankruptcy concludes when the trustee sells the debtor's property, distributes the cash to the creditors and discharges the remaining debt. The discharge extinguishes the debtor's remaining personal liability on the debt. Certain items are nondischargeable and thus unaffected by the bankruptcy. Nondischargeable debts include:

- Alimony and child support
- Most tax obligations
- Most student loans
- Liability for damages resulting from willful or malicious acts

Creditors can ask the court to deny an individual debtor a discharge. The grounds for denial of discharge are extremely narrow and requests for denial are rarely granted. Grounds for denial include:

- The debtor fails to adequately explain the loss of assets
- The debtor perjured himself or herself or failed to obey lawful orders of the court
- The debtor fraudulently transfers, conceals or destroys property that should be in the estate

Because a secured creditor has rights that permit him or her to seize pledged property, a debtor may want to reaffirm a debt even after it has been discharged if the debtor wants to keep the property. A reaffirmation is an agreement between the debtor and the secured creditor that the creditor will not exercise his or her right to take back the asset so long as the debtor makes payments.

A debtor must wait six years before he or she can file for Chapter 7 again.

CHAPTER 13

Chapter 13 bankruptcy is often referred to as a "wage-earner plan," because it is generally used by people with stable incomes who want to repay at least some of their debts but are currently unable to do so. A debtor may file Chapter 13 bankruptcy if his or her financial crisis is temporary and he or she thinks that his or her income will grow enough in the next few years to pay off all debts. The main advantage to Chapter 13 is that the debtor is allowed to keep his or her property while a court-approved repayment plan is in effect. However, only individuals with less than $250,000 in unsecured debts and less than $350,000 in secured debts are eligible to file a Chapter 13 bankruptcy. Corporations and partnerships cannot file Chapter 13 bankruptcies. In addition, the debtor must have a job or prove to the court that he or she has the ability to earn stable income.

STEP 1: PETITION

The petition required for a Chapter 13 bankruptcy is similar to that described above for Chapter 7. The debtor provides the court with the following:

- Lists of all creditors, including the amount and nature of claims
- The source, amount and frequency of debtor income
- Lists of all property
- Detailed descriptions of the debtor's monthly living expenses, including food, clothing, shelter, utilities, taxes, transportation and medical care

STEP 2: STAY

Filing a Chapter 13 petition automatically stays most actions against the debtor. So long as the stay is in effect, creditors generally cannot start or continue lawsuits, garnishment actions, or even phone the debtor demanding repayment. Chapter 13 also has a special stay provision that prohibits creditors from collecting consumer debt owed to the debtor by a third person.

STEP 3: PLAN

Within 15 working days of filing a Chapter 13 bankruptcy, the debtor presents a plan to the court that spells out how he or she proposes to pay off debts over a three-year period or, by permission, a five-year period. The plan must provide for the full payment of claims entitled to priority. For reasons of public policy, the Bankruptcy Code has several categories of unsecured claims that have priority over other unsecured claims including:

- Costs of administering the bankruptcy
- Employees' wages, salaries and commissions
- Contributions to employee benefit plans
- Deposits accepted by the debtor for personal items or services that the debtor did not deliver
- Taxes

STEP 4: CREDITORS MEETING

A creditors meeting is usually held about 20 to 40 days after the petition is filed. The debtor and trustee must attend the conference, but creditors have the option to attend. Trustee and creditors can question the debtor about financial affairs and terms of the plan. Any problems with the plan are usually solved during or shortly after this meeting.

STEP 5: CONFIRMATION HEARING

After the creditors meeting, at a bankruptcy hearing, the bankruptcy court determines whether the plan is feasible and meets the confirmation standards the bankruptcy code sets. Creditors are allowed to object to confirmation. The most common objections are that the debtor has not pledged sufficient disposable income to the plan or that the creditors receive less than they would if the debtors assets were liquidated in a Chapter 7 proceeding.

For most plans in Minnesota, the Bankruptcy Court allows a five-year repayment plan. The court occasionally reduces the size of some of the dischargeable debts. During this three- or five-year period, a portion of the debtor's paycheck goes to a court-appointed trustee who divides the money among the debtor's creditors.

If approved by the Bankruptcy Court, the plan prevents a debtor's creditors from garnishing wages or repossessing property.

STEP 6: DISCHARGE

A Chapter 13 debtor is entitled to a discharge if he or she successfully completes all payments under an approved plan. The discharge releases the debtor from all debts provided for or disallowed under the plan. Creditors provided for under the plan may not start or continue actions against the debtor to collect a discharged obligation.

ADVANTAGES OF CHAPTER 13 OVER CHAPTER 7

Filing a Chapter 13 bankruptcy has advantages over a Chapter 7 liquidation. Unlike a Chapter 7 bankruptcy, there is not a six-year waiting period before the debtor can file bankruptcy again. Thus, with only a few exceptions, the debtor can file a Chapter 7 bankruptcy at any time after filing Chapter 13 bankruptcy. This means that if the debtor finds that he or she cannot make the payments specified in a Chapter 13 bankruptcy plan, he or she can still act to discharge debts through a Chapter 7 liquidation.

The nondischargeable debts under a Chapter 13 bankruptcy are generally the same as the nondischargeable debts in a Chapter 7 bankruptcy. However, a Chapter 13 bankruptcy allows the debtor to discharge a few more types of debts than does a Chapter 7 bankruptcy.

If the debtor owns an unincorporated business, such as a freelance consulting business, she can continue to own and operate the business under a Chapter 13 plan. Under a Chapter 7 liquidation, a Bankruptcy Court may order that such a business or its assets be sold. Also, the automatic stay of a Chapter 13 bankruptcy protects any co-signers of consumer debts, whereas a Chapter 7 offers only very limited protection of others who may share the debtor's obligation.

Finally, certain homeowners may prefer a Chapter 13 bankruptcy, because in many instances it allows them to make up past payments on their mortgage. When someone falls behind in making mortgage payments or is in actual default, a lender quite often "accelerates" the payments. For a debtor in this situation, filing a Chapter 13 bankruptcy may allow her to "decelerate" or reduce those monthly payments and may even reinstate the mortgage by wiping out a prior default. However, the same advice given above to a homeowner considering a Chapter 7 bankruptcy also applies here. If saving a house is the primary reason for filing bankruptcy, it is wise to talk through all the possibilities with an attorney, because the laws governing this area are extremely complicated and it is easy to make a costly misstep.

CONVERSION

The Bankruptcy Code allows a debtor to convert a Chapter 7 case to Chapter 13 or vice versa as long as the debtor meets the eligibility requirements of the new chapter and the case has not previously been converted from the new chapter. In other words, the debtor is not allowed to repeatedly convert the case from one chapter to another.

INVOLUNTARY BANKRUPTCY

Unlike the types of situations described above, where the debtor decides whether to file bankruptcy, in an involuntary bankruptcy creditors force the debtor into bankruptcy. Under certain conditions, creditors can petition the Bankruptcy Court to initiate a Chapter 7 or 11 (but not a Chapter 13) bankruptcy against a debtor. The court will only accept such a petition if it is signed by at least three creditors who are owed a total of at least $5000 in unsecured debt. If a debtor has fewer than 12 unsecured creditors, however, just one unsecured creditor owed at least $5000 can file an involuntary bankruptcy petition.

Involuntary bankruptcy is rare, but if someone does file a petition against a debtor in Bankruptcy Court, he or she has an opportunity to file an answer to the petition and refute any charges made against him or her by creditors in the petition. If the judge sides with the debtor, the court dismisses the petition and can make the creditors pay reasonable attorney's fees and any money the debtor loses in defending the case. In addition, if the judge decides that the petition was filed in bad faith the court may also award the debtor punitive damages.

EFFECTS OF DECLARING BANKRUPTCY

The old adage that it is better to know how to swim before jumping into deep water applies to anyone considering filing bankruptcy.

POOR CREDIT RATING

Consumer laws allow credit agencies to list on reports of a person's credit history all of his or her bankruptcy filings in the preceding ten years. This means that mortgage companies, banks, credit card companies, landlords, employers and all others who can legally obtain a copy of a person's credit report will know about his or her troubled financial past. Filing bankruptcy can make it difficult to obtain credit for ten years.

CREDITOR SCRUTINY

One of the first events in a bankruptcy is a meeting between the debtor and all his or her creditors. At this meeting, the creditors and a court-appointed trustee are allowed to examine all of the debtor's financial records, such as bank statements and loan documents, and ask questions about how money has been spent. For anyone with anything unsavory or illegal to hide, such as gambling debts with a bookie, a bankruptcy proceeding can be incriminating.

COST

Understandably, bankruptcy attorneys are very careful about a clients' ability to pay legal bills. Most bankruptcy attorneys usually collect enough money in advance from their near-bankrupt clients to handle a typical bankruptcy filing. This may be more than some clients can pay, especially if there is any contest with creditors. In addition, the trustee in charge of a bankruptcy case is paid by commission, a percentage of the money that he or she distributes to pay creditors.

OTHER FORMS OF BANKRUPTCY

There are three other kinds of bankruptcy filings that are not discussed more fully in this chapter because of their limited relevance to consumers. Knowing about them can help one better understand bankruptcy options:

CHAPTER 9

Chapter 9 is a very rare form of bankruptcy available only to municipalities.

CHAPTER 11

Chapter 11 is available for corporations, partnerships, and individuals but is mostly used by troubled corporations and partnerships. Chapter 11 allows the debtor to remain in operation while being sheltered from some of its debts.

FARM BANKRUPTCIES

Chapter 12 is available only to family farmers and is designed to allow farmers to stay in business while attempting to pay off their debts. Chapter 12 offers several advantages over other bankruptcy chapters because it recognizes the seasonal nature of most agricultural income, the difficulty of predicting in advance how much a farmer will profit from a crop, and the fact that most farmers need much more credit than do most individuals. Chapter 12 was originally scheduled to be repealed on October 1, 1993, but the repeal date was pushed back to October 1, 1998.

TRANSFERS TO AVOID LOSING AN ASSET IN BANKRUPTCY

Some transfers that are valid outside the context of bankruptcy are invalid in bankruptcy. The Bankruptcy Code empowers a bankruptcy trustee to invalidate certain transfers made prior to a bankruptcy filing.

FRAUDULENT CONVEYANCES

The Uniform Fraudulent Transfer Act is designed to remove any temptation a debtor may have to hide property (by giving it to a relative, for example) before declaring bankruptcy. Any transfer of the debtor's assets made within 90 days (or one year if a relative or business associate is involved) of filing bankruptcy is carefully scrutinized by the Bankruptcy Court. If the court determines that the debtor attempted to defraud creditors by selling property at a below-market price, the court can order that property or other assets be given over to the trustee. The court cannot recover anything sold at a reasonable market value before a bankruptcy filing under the rules of the Uniform Fraudulent Transfer Act.

PREFERENCES

A preference occurs when a debtor treats one creditor more favorably than another. For instance, if a debtor with only $100 owes $100 each to creditors A and B and pays A completely, leaving nothing for B, then A has received a preference. Bankruptcy condemns preferences if the following conditions exist:

- Transfer is for the benefit of a creditor
- Transfer is made for debt owed prior to the initiation of bankruptcy
- Debtor is insolvent at the time of transfer
- Transfer is made 90 days before filing of the bankruptcy or one year if made to an insider such as a relative or director of a corporate debtor. Creditors receiving preferences can be forced to return them to the debtor's estate.

COLLECTION AGENCIES AND THE LAW

Although not a part of Bankruptcy Code, laws regulating collection agencies are usually of concern to anyone experiencing financial difficulties. Both state and federal laws limit the kinds of activities that a collection agency can engage in as it tries to collect a debt. These laws only apply to third-party collection agencies and not to in-house collections. That is, if a creditor tries on its own to induce its delinquent accounts to pay their overdue bills it is not required to follow the laws governing collection agencies. But if a creditor turns collection matters over to a collection agency, the collection agency's employees must follow the rules. Laws regulating debt collection agencies are discussed more fully in the Consumer Protection Chapter.

ALTERNATIVES TO BANKRUPTCY

Anyone in financial trouble has undoubtedly received many letters from creditors demanding payment on debts owed. Even a very demanding creditor may have a change of heart once a debtor mentions the possibility of filing bankruptcy, because creditors know that bankruptcy means that they may only get a fraction of what is owed them.
Anyone confident that his or her financial problems are only temporary may want to consider asking major creditors to accept reduced payments for a short period or asking for a short delay in making payments. Provided that the debtor has not already given creditors reason to doubt his or her sincerity, e.g., by completely ignoring their letters or by consistently breaking promises, chances are good that creditors will agree on one of these plans.
As mentioned above, creditors know that bankruptcy means they will probably get just a small fraction of the total sum owed them. Creditors also know that if they sue to collect their money, they undergo the hassle of going to a judge to get a court order to garnish the debtor's wages. This is time-consuming and costly. All these factors make it more likely that a creditor will agree to a repayment plan.
Many creditors can be understanding if approached with a reduced or delayed payment plan accurately spelling out the debtor's financial situation and showing that the debtor is trying to spread out his or her meager resources in a way that tries to please everyone. A consumer credit counselor can help set up such a plan. Credit counselors can help to analyze and organize one's finances to set up a deferred or reduced payment plan. In a typical case, a credit counselor devises a repayment plan that is then described in a form letter to be mailed to the debtor's major creditors. There are both advantages and disadvantages to using credit counselors, however. On the plus side, creditors who see that a debtor has taken the effort to consult with a credit advisor may be more likely to accept a repayment plan because seeing a credit counselor shows that the debtor is serious about getting out of debt. But credit counseling services also charge fees for their work, which may be more than an already-stressed budget can handle. However, there are some nonprofit agencies that offer credit counseling for a sliding-scale fee.

B A N K R U P T C Y   L A W :   I N D I V I D U A L

Iannacone Law Office
101 East Fifth Street
Suite 1614
St. Paul, MN 55101

Phone: (612) 224-3361
Fax: (612) 297-6187

MICHAEL J.
IANNACONE

MICHAEL J. IANNACONE: Mr. Iannacone handles bankruptcy cases under Chapters 7, 11, 12, and 13 workouts and collections, representing debtors or lenders and serving as a Bankruptcy Trustee. He is appointed by the Department of Justice, Office of the United States Trustee to act as a Trustee in approximately 600 cases per year and as operating Trustee in Chapter 11 cases.

Education: JD 1975, William Mitchell; BA 1970, Harvard University.

Admitted: 1975 Minnesota; 1975 U.S. Dist. Ct. (MN).

Employment History: Mr. Iannacone has been a sole practitioner in St. Paul since 1976.

Representative Clients: Mr. Iannacone has served as Chapter 11 Trustee for the French Accent; Chapter 7 Trustee for Schaak Electronics, Hoffmann Electric, and Kullberg-White; represented debtor in *In re Substad*, which upheld exempt status of over $200,000 of IRA funds; and represented farmers and lenders during the farm crises of the mid-1980s.

Professional Associations: National Assn. of Bankruptcy Trustees; RCBA; MSBA; ABA.

Community Involvement: Southeast Metro Sharks swim meets (Head Timer).

Firm: The Iannacone Law Office has one associate attorney, Heather L. Iannacone, who practices primarily in trustee litigation and administration.

Extensive Experience In:
• Bankruptcy
• Loan Workouts & Restructuring
• Asset Protection

Bankruptcy Law: Individual

Prescott & Pearson, P.A.
403 Eighth Avenue NW
P.O. Box 120088
New Brighton, MN 55112

Phone: (612) 633-2757
Fax: (612) 633-7562

JACK L. PRESCOTT

JACK L. PRESCOTT: Mr. Prescott practices exclusively in bankruptcy debtor law, with 90 percent of his practice focusing on consumer cases; he also deals with small business companies. He has handled 40,000 bankruptcy cases since 1951 and currently has the highest percentage of all filed cases in Minnesota (more than any other office). Having acted as a municipal judge for 12 years, Mr. Prescott has worked on both sides of a lawsuit. His long history of lecturing to other lawyers on consumer banking demonstrates his knowledge in this area. In addition, he has lectured on consumer bankruptcy for Minnesota Continuing Legal Education for several years. Mr. Prescott has established a policy of nothing down (except clerk fee) and an affordable payment plan on consumer cases.

Education: LLB, JD 1947-51, St. Paul College; BSL 1945-46, Hamline University, 1946-47 University of Minnesota.

Admitted: 1951 Minnesota.

Employment History: Currently President/Owner, Prescott & Pearson, P.A.; 12 years as municipal judge, New Brighton, MN.

Representative Clients: 3,000 consumer debtors filed in each of the last several years.

Professional Associations: MSBA (Bankruptcy Section); RCBA.

Firm: Prescott and Pearson, P.A., consists of three attorneys, six paralegals and seven clerical persons. The firm provides many years of experience, especially in consumer Chapter 7 and Chapter 13 cases, to its clients.

EMPLOYMENT LAW: INDIVIDUAL

Reviewed and edited by Leading Minnesota Attorneys Daniel J. Heuel of Muir, Heuel, Carlson & Spelhaug, P.A.; Donald E. Horton of Horton and Associates; Gerald T. Laurie of Lapp, Laurie, Libra, Abramson & Thomson, Chartered; and Clarence A. Anderson, supervising reemployment insurance judge with the Minnesota Department of Economic Security.

Workers enjoy many rights designed to make the workplace safe and free from illegal discrimination and harassment. This chapter outlines some of the more important federal and state laws that govern the legal relationships and problems that develop between an employer and employee.

THE EMPLOYMENT RELATIONSHIP

Many of the rights a worker enjoys turn on the legal relationship that exists between the worker and his or her employer.

INDEPENDENT CONTRACTOR VERSUS EMPLOYEE

When a worker gets paid to do a task or provide a service for another person, the worker is either an independent contractor or an employee. The distinction is important both for the business and the worker, but it is not always clear. An employer who hires someone as an independent contractor can avoid many tax and record-keeping requirements. For a worker, the classification determines the benefits a worker is entitled to, whether the worker can file a workers' compensation claim, and whether the worker is protected by federal and state wage and hour regulations. Employees enjoy substantially more protection in the workplace than do independent contractors.

Whether a worker is an independent contractor or an employee is based on the work performed, not the worker's title. The more control an employer has over a worker, the more likely it is the worker is an employee. The more a worker acts like an independent business enterprise, the more likely the worker is an independent contractor. In some cases, the status is clear: a worker who arrives at a set time every day, is trained by the employer, uses the boss's tools or equipment, and is paid by the hour, week or month is most likely an employee. Someone who works for more than one company at a time, can set his or her own hours, and realizes a profit or risks a loss is most likely an independent contractor.

A worker or an employer who is unsure about the legal status of the employment can ask the Internal Revenue Service, the Minnesota Department of Revenue or the Minnesota Department of Jobs and Training for an opinion based on the respective agency's guidelines. Guidelines vary from agency to agency, and one agency may classify someone as an employee even though another considers the same employee an independent contractor.

EMPLOYMENT-AT-WILL

The state of Minnesota recognizes the traditional rule of employment-at-will. This means that, unless there is an agreement to the contrary, an employer can discharge an employee at any time for no reason or for any reason other than an illegal reason. It also means that an employee can resign at any time, for any reason, with or without giving notice. The implications of this relationship are far-reaching. Employers do not need a good reason to fire someone. So long as an employee is not fired for an illegal reason, such as racial or gender discrimination, even a silly or unfounded reason is enough to fire an employee. Similarly, an employee is free to leave an employer for any reason at all, even if by doing so he or she greatly inconveniences the employer.

Most workers in Minnesota are at-will employees. Generally, all employees are at-will unless the employer does something to change the status of the relationship. There are several ways an employer can alter the relationship. An employer might enter into an oral or written contract guaranteeing to employ someone for a specific period of time or promising to terminate the employee only for specified reasons. An employee handbook or collective bargaining agreement can limit the employer's right to terminate employees. An employer can inadvertently limit his or her right to fire an employee if, by his or her actions, he or she gives the employee reason to believe the job will continue. For example, if an employer promises a job to someone from out of state and that person moves to Minnesota specifically to take the job, the employment relationship is probably not at-will because the employee has gone to the trouble and expense of moving after reasonably relying on the promise of new employment.

GOVERNMENT ADMINISTERED BENEFITS

Three programs administered by the state and federal governments are of primary interest to workers: Unemployment Compensation Insurance, Workers' Compensation Insurance, and Social Security. Each of these programs determines a worker's benefits according to the terms and conditions of employment.

REEMPLOYMENT (FORMERLY KNOWN AS UNEMPLOYMENT) INSURANCE

Reemployment insurance provides benefits to employees who are laid off, fired, or forced to leave their jobs. Most employees are covered by reemployment insurance, a program administered by the state and funded by employer contributions.

Application

Reemployment benefits are not automatic; the worker must apply for them from the Minnesota Department of Economic Security. After gathering information about an applicant, the department makes an initial determination whether the person is eligible to receive benefits. If the department's decision is that the employee is eligible, the department informs the former employer. Because the former employer pays the benefits, the employer has the right to know what the former employee told the department and has an opportunity to present its side of the story.

Eligibility

Not everyone who leaves a job is eligible to receive reemployment benefits. To be eligible to receive reemployment benefits, the employee must have made at least $1000 in wages in any one calendar quarter. The employment must end either by the employer being fired for a reason other than misconduct, or by the employee quitting because of a good reason caused by the employer. There are several statutory exceptions to disqualification including quitting due to serious illness after making reasonable efforts to retain the employment and quitting to accept better employment and then losing the new job.

Independent contractors are not covered by reemployment insurance.

An applicant cannot receive benefits if any one of the following conditions applies:

- The applicant is a student hired by the educational institution in which he or she was enrolled
- The applicant is fired for misconduct
- The applicant refuses an offer to work again for the former employer, if the offered work is suiitable or if the refusal is without good cause.
- The applicant fails to apply for or accept suitable work
- The applicant quits for any reason other than an illegal or otherwise intolerable work environment

Because employers and employees often have different ideas of what constitutes a reasonable work environment, the issue in many disputes over reemployment claims is whether the employer created an intolerable workplace environment. Only certain kinds of employer actions give someone a legitimate reason to quit a job and still collect unemployment benefits. Some valid reasons are: sexual harassment by an employer or inaction by an employer who was informed of instances of sexual harassment; a substantial cut in pay or benefits; drastic changes in working conditions or hours without an employee's consent; and requiring an employee to break the law or work under obviously unsafe conditions.

Conditions of employment that generally do not let an employee collect Reemployment benefits include: a demotion or other change in management structure that leads to a modest decrease in wages or benefits; disagreements over management policy; and reasonable changes in workplace hours or employee regulations.

Benefits

If the department decides that an applicant is eligible to receive benefits, he or she receives a portion of their previous salary up to a maximum ceiling determined by the average statewide salary calculated each year. Benefits are paid for up to 26 times the claimant's weekly benefit amount or until an applicant has received one-third of his or her former salary, whichever is sooner. Finding a part-time or temporary job will not necessarily prevent someone from receiving unemployment benefits if he or she continues to look for permanent work. The recipient keeps $50 or 25 percent of his or her weekly income, whichever is more. Unemployment benefits are reduced by any income in excess of $50 or 25 percent.

WORKERS' COMPENSATION

Workers' Compensation provides benefits to employees injured in the workplace, regardless of whose negligence causes the injury. With few a exceptions, all Minnesota employees are covered by the Minnesota Workers' Compensation Act.

The benefits available to workers include death benefits, permanent and temporary total disability, permanent and temporary partial disability, and medical and related expenses. The benefit amounts are determined by state guidelines and can be as high as two-thirds of a worker's salary at the time of the injury.

SOCIAL SECURITY

Social Security provides benefits for retired workers, including full or part-time wage or salary workers; self-employed persons, farm workers; members of the United States Armed Services; employees of private nonprofit organizations; most federal, state, and local government employees; and most domestic workers. The usual age for first receiving Social Security benefits is age 65; however, a worker has the option of initiating benefits at age 62. The amount of each monthly check varies depending on how much the worker made each year. The higher his or her pay, the higher the benefits, up to a maximum dollar amount. Social Security also provides disabled persons with benefits. To be eligible, a person must be unable to engage in any gainful employment.

CIVIL RIGHTS IN THE WORKPLACE

Four major federal laws–the Civil Rights Acts of 1964 and 1991, the Age Discrimination in Employment Act of 1967, and the Americans with Disabilities Act of 1990–protect the rights of American workers to be free from workplace discrimination. Minnesota workers also have additional protection under the Minnesota Human Rights Act.

Many federal civil rights laws apply only to employers with a minimum number of employees. The federal Americans with Disabilities Act, for example, only applies to employers with 15 or more employees after July 26, 1994. In most cases, the Minnesota Human Rights Act applies to all Minnesota employers who have one or more employees, except close relatives. In addition, the Minnesota act covers more types of discrimination than do the federal laws, such as marital status, sexual orientation and receipt of public assistance.

IN GENERAL

Most employment discrimination is outlawed by two major civil rights acts passed by Congress in 1964 and 1991 and by the Minnesota Human Rights Act. Through a combination of these laws, Minnesota workers are protected against discrimination based on race, color, creed, religion, national origin, gender, sexual orientation, marital status, status with regard to public assistance, membership or activity in a local commission, age, or disability.

People frequently refer to "Title VII" rights when they are talking about a particular section of the Civil Rights Act of 1964. Title VII prohibits discrimination in a wide number of employment areas including hiring, firing, recruitment, transfers, promotions, testing, layoffs, recalls, fringe benefits, training, apprenticeship programs and job advertisements. Title VII also specifically prohibits retaliation against a person who files a charge of discrimination, participates in an investigation of discrimination or opposes an unlawful employment practice.

Under certain extremely limited circumstances these civil rights acts allow employers to base their employment decisions or practices on a person's marital status, gender, etc., if the employer can demonstrate a truly legitimate need. For example, it is not impermissible gender discrimination to refuse to hire a man to be an attendant in a women's locker room. Religious institutions can refuse to hire individuals based on their religious beliefs, but only for positions that are directly related to the performance of religious duties. Religious institutions are generally not allowed to discriminate when hiring individuals for secular tasks such as secretarial or janitorial work.

Certain employers, such as police departments, can base employment decisions on an applicant's physical abilities. Some pre-employment exams are allowed under Minnesota law if they measure skills that are truly essential for an applicant to have in order to perform a particular job and are not applied in a selective or discriminatory way. Lawyers, for example, must pass a bar exam before they can practice law, and a company hiring secretaries can give applicants typing exams.

Proving discrimination in the workplace depends on each situation's specifics. It is generally easier to prove discrimination from a repeated behavior pattern rather than an isolated incident. For example, a strong case of racial discrimination could be made against an employer if members of a certain class of people are held to a higher standard than others.

In addition, any documented evidence showing an employer is prejudiced against a class of people can strengthen a discrimination case. If an employer makes statements such as "blacks don't take orders well" or "women aren't capable of making tough management decisions," this will likely increase the chances of proving discrimination, especially if the statements are made repeatedly and in the presence of witnesses.

A person who feels that he or she has been unfairly discriminated against or harassed in the workplace can file a complaint with the Minnesota Department of Human Rights or the federal Equal Employment Opportunity Commission (EEOC). The Minnesota Department of Human Rights enforces the Minnesota Human Rights Act, and the EEOC enforces federal civil rights in the workplace. When a person files a complaint with either of these agencies, that agency cross-files with the other agency. A victim of discrimination has 300 days to file a complaint with the EEOC or one year to file a complaint with the Department of Human Rights after the alleged discriminatory incident occurs. The victim of discrimination can also hire a private attorney to pursue a claim against an employer.

AGE DISCRIMINATION

The Age Discrimination in Employment Act (ADEA) expands Title VII prohibitions against age discrimination. Most employers cannot enforce mandatory retirement policies, except under a few very specific circumstances where age is truly a qualification for doing a particular job, such as firefighting, police work or flying airplanes. Anyone age 40 or older working for an employer with 20 or more employees is protected by the ADEA and cannot be retired against his or her will, regardless of age, as long as he or she can do the job. Any Minnesota employer employing fewer than 20 employees is prohibited by state law from discriminating based on age, but such an employer can force an employee 70 or older to retire.

DISCRIMINATION AGAINST PERSONS WITH DISABILITIES

The Americans with Disabilities Act (ADA) is a federal law prohibiting discrimination based on physical and mental ability. The ADA also requires employers to make reasonable accommodations for physically or mentally disabled employees, including modifying facilities and work schedules and providing special training. Using pre-employment tests that identify and exclude disabled applicants is permissible only where the tests are unequivocally job-related.

The ADA does not change in any way an employer's right to hire people who have the skills to perform a job's "essential duties". The ADA makes it illegal to refuse to hire an applicant or to fire a current employee who lacks physical or mental abilities that are not essential to the job. For example, an employer cannot reject a person with epilepsy who has applied for a job as a daycare provider merely because the applicant's epilepsy prevents her from having a driver's license. Just because the applicant could not take children to a hospital in emergencies is not a valid reason to discriminate against the epileptic applicant, since occasionally driving a child to a medical clinic or hospital is not an "essential" task of a daycare provider.

An employer required to comply with the ADA must do whatever is reasonable to accommodate a person's disability, including modifying work schedules, changing the work environment, buying or modifying special equipment, or reassigning to another position a disabled employee who can no longer do a job's "essential duties." A "reasonable accommodation" for an employer to make is one that does not place an undue burden on the employer.

The ADA only protects from discrimination those people with permanent conditions that limit a major life activity. Thus, an employee who has a sprained ankle that is expected to heal fully is not protected under the ADA, even though that employee is disabled for a period of time. A person with a permanent disabling condition that is controlled by drugs, physical therapy or by some other treatment, however, is covered by the ADA. For example, an epileptic whose seizures are controlled by medication is protected from discrimination by the ADA. People with AIDS are covered by the ADA. The ADA also prohibits discriminating against individuals who have completed or are still participating in drug rehabilitation programs. However, an applicant or employee currently using illegal drugs is not protected by the ADA.

SEXUAL HARASSMENT

Everyone, male or female, has the right to be free from sexual harassment in the workplace. Sexual harassment can take many forms:

• Someone says something sexual about a coworker's appearance
• An employer enforces a mandatory dress code that provokes others to make sexually explicit comments
• Someone makes unwanted sexual contact
• Someone connects a condition of the job, such as a raise, with sexual contact
• Someone makes sexual jokes or explicit sexual comments that embarrass a coworker
• Someone displays or passes around pornographic pictures

Sexual harassment is punishable as an illegal form of sex discrimination under Title VII of the Civil Rights Act of 1964 and under the Minnesota Human Rights Act. Sexual harassment is illegal if participation in any of the above activities is required to get or keep a job, to be promoted or to qualify for benefits, or if it makes it harder for a worker to do his or her job by creating a hostile environment.

Unwelcome behavior must be both undesirable and offensive to be considered sexual harassment. Of these two criteria, the most problematic is determining what kind of behavior is offensive. Because of the diversity of sexual attitudes in this country, what is sexually offensive to one person may just be harmless sexual banter to another. The law uses the "reasonable person" standard to determine what is offensive, if a reasonable person would find an action offensive, then it is offensive.

While determining what kind of behavior constitutes sexual harassment is an inexact science, some general descriptions of sexual harassment can be made. A single, or very occasional, sexual joke or sexual comment is not sexual harassment unless the comment unequivocally offers workplace advancement in return for sexual favors. Unwanted touching of someone else's body is sexual harassment, as is the repeated telling of lewd or obscene jokes that make an employee uncomfortable. A case for sexual harassment is strengthened if the person doing the touching or telling the dirty jokes has been repeatedly told that he or she makes the workplace uncomfortable. A case for sexual harassment is weakened if the person claiming harassment participates in the joke-telling or similar activity. Comments and conduct by members of management are also scrutinized more closely than similar acts by coworkers.

In addition to laws designed to give victims a civil remedy against sexual harassment, criminal laws provide remedies against the most serious forms of unwanted sexual contact. If a harasser's behavior crosses the line into assault, battery or rape, the victim can file criminal charges against the perpetrator.

Anyone fired or forced to leave a job because of sexual harassment may be entitled to receive unemployment insurance benefits while searching for a new job.

PREGNANCY DISCRIMINATION

Title VII protects pregnant workers and pregnant job applicants from discrimination. Employers cannot refuse to hire a woman because she is pregnant, fire a woman because she is pregnant, take away benefits or accrued seniority because a woman takes maternity leave, or fire or refuse to hire a woman who has an abortion.

Generally, an employer must treat pregnant women the same as other workers who cannot perform their jobs for short periods of time. Thus, if an employer allows employees to take a leave for a broken leg or short-term illness, he or she must allow pregnant women to take a leave under the same terms and conditions. Pregnancy leave is also protected under the Family and Medical Leave Act discussed below.

OTHER WORKPLACE RIGHTS AND RESPONSIBILITIES

WAGES AND HOURS

As of September 1, 1997, the federal minimum wage for adult workers age 18 and over is $5.15 per hour. Exceptions to the minimum wage law are given for some minors, disabled workers and trainees. Employers must pay at least the minimum wage, even to employees who earn tips. Employers cannot force employees to share their tips with other workers or managers, although employees may do so voluntarily. With few exceptions, employers must pay hourly employees one and a half times their regular rate for all hours worked in a week in excess of 40 hours.

Certain salaried workers are exempt from minimum wage standards and overtime regulations. To be exempt, an employee must be in an executive, administrative or professional position and receive at least $250 each week in salary or fee. The employee must either supervise at least two other workers, manage an office or a business operation, be a skilled artistic performer or a teacher or work in a profession requiring advanced knowledge, such as engineering.

Students who are 16 or 17 years old cannot work on days before school is scheduled between 11:30 p.m. and 4:30 a.m. Minors 14 and 15 years old cannot work between the hours of 7 p.m. and 7 a.m. while school is in session and from 9 p.m. to 7 a.m. during summer vacation, and they cannot work more than three hours per day or 18 hours per week during the school year. Minors 15 or younger working as models, actors or performers, doing chores such as babysitting and housework for others, or working for their parents are exempt from these time-of-work restrictions. Also exempt from these time-of-work restrictions are newspaper carriers, if they are at least 11 years old, and those working in agricultural jobs with parental permission.

SUBSTANCE ABUSE IN THE WORKPLACE

The Minnesota Human Rights Act does, under some conditions, protect alcoholics and drug addicts from discrimination. The protection is not absolute; an alcoholic or drug addict can be disciplined or fired if the drug or alcohol addiction prevents the addict from performing essential job duties, or if the addiction endangers the safety of others.

Under certain circumstances, employers in Minnesota can compel employees to pass drug and alcohol tests as a condition of employment. These tests must not be given in a discriminatory way, and if passing a drug or alcohol test is a job requirement, then all employees performing that job must subject to the testing requirement.

An employer may test an employee for drugs and alcohol only under the following conditions:

- Reasonable suspicion: when an employer notices obvious signs (slurred speech, glazed eyes, etc.) that an employee is under the influence of drugs or alcohol;

when an employee injures herself or another worker while on the job or has an accident while operating a vehicle to perform a work-related task; when an employee has unmistakably violated workplace rules on drugs or alcohol while operating an employer's machinery, equipment, or vehicle
* Safety-sensitive positions: when an employee performs a task in which drug or alcohol impairment directly affects the safety of other workers or the general public
* Routine physical exams: when conducting a routine physical exam, provided that giving such an exam is directly related to job performance. In addition, such a test cannot be required more than once a year and employees must be given at least two weeks' written notice of the exam
* Treatment program follow-up: at any time in the two years after an employee completes a drug or alcohol treatment program, provided an employee benefit plan covered the treatment or if the employer directed the employee to complete the treatment

Any such testing must be done in accordance with a written policy, and the policy must be made available in advance to all employees. Also, under the law, an individual who fails a substance test must be given a chance to go through rehabilitation before being fired.

PARENTING, FAMILY AND MEDICAL LEAVE
Both the State of Minnesota and the federal government require certain employers to provide parenting, family and medical leave to qualified employees. The federal law in this area preempts state law only where the federal law provides greater benefits. In areas for which Minnesota provides greater benefits, Minnesota law is controlling. Accordingly, it pays to be familiar with both laws.

Federal Law
The Family and Medical Leave Act of 1993 (FMLA) is a federal law that allows qualified employees to take up to 12 weeks of unpaid leave to attend to family matters, including health emergencies. Under the act, a qualified employee may take an unpaid leave following the birth or adoption of a child, after acquiring a foster child, to care for an immediate family member with a serious health condition, or to care for his or her own serious health condition. Men and women are equally entitled to take these leaves.

Not every worker is qualified to take these leaves of absence. A person must be a full-time employee of a company with 50 or more employees and have worked for the company at least 12 months. In addition, an employee must have worked at the company for at least 1,250 hours during the 12 months immediately prior to taking a leave under the FMLA.

Under the act, an employer must maintain the health benefits that an employee was receiving at the time a leave begins, during periods of unpaid FMLA leave at the same level and in the same manner as if the employee had continued to work. Under most circumstances, an employee may elect or the employer may require the use of any accrued paid leave for periods of unpaid leave under the FMLA. The employee is not entitled to accrue benefits such as vacation time or sick leave during a leave under the FMLA.

When the leave is foreseeable, an employee must provide the employer with at least 30 days notice of the need for leave. If the leave is not foreseeable, then the notice must be given as soon as it is practical. An employer may require medical certification of a serious health condition from the employee and may require periodic reports during the period of leave of the employee's status and intent to return to work. In addition, an employer may require a fitness-for-duty certification upon return to work in appropriate situations.

When an employee returns from a leave under the FMLA, the employee is entitled to be restored to the same job the employee left when the leave began. If the same job is not available, the employer must place the employee in an equivalent job with equivalent pay, benefits, duties and responsibilities. Any benefits accrued by the employee at the time of the leave have to stay with the employee. Under the act, employers are prohibited from discriminating against or interfering with employees who take FMLA leaves.

Minnesota Law
Under the Minnesota Family Leave Act, employers with 20 or more employees are required to provide qualified employees with up to six weeks unpaid vacation time for the birth or adoption of a child. During the employee's absence, the employer must make insurance benefits available to the employee, although the employee can be required to make the payments for that insurance. Upon return, the employee is entitled to his or her previous job or a comparable position. A worker choosing not to return to work at the end of a leave period may be considered to have voluntarily quit and be denied unemployment benefits. Employers with 20 or more employees must allow employees to use their own accrued sick, disability or medical leave to care for a sick or injured child for such reasonable period as necessary to care for the child.

Privacy
Employees' right to privacy while at work is a hotly debated issue today as increasing numbers of employers turn to searches, surveillance and eavesdropping in an attempt to better monitor their employees' activities. The law in this area is evolving and still largely unsettled, but it is fair to say that an employee surrenders some of his or her right to privacy at the workplace door. An employer has far greater legal right to monitor employees than the government has to monitor citizens.

The controlling factor courts look to in deciding if an employee has a right of privacy is whether an employee's expectation of privacy in a particular situation is reasonable. For example, the expectation of privacy is more reasonable for items in a locked desk drawer than for items left out on a desk. Similarly, the expectation is more reasonable for private phone calls made on a pay phone than for work-related calls made on the employer's phone.

The reasonable expectation standard is not a very strong guarantor of employee privacy. An employer can dramatically expand his or her right to searches, monitoring and surveillance simply by giving notice to employees. Once an employee receives notice that the employer reserves the right to monitor calls, search offices, read electronic mail or film the workplace, there is very little reasonable expectation of privacy.

Leave of Absence
Under Minnesota law, all employers are required to provide paid voting leave during the morning of regularly scheduled state primary or general elections, presidential primary, or election to fill a vacancy in the United States House of Representatives or Senate. All employers are required to provide unpaid leave so that employees can serve on juries, testify in trial or serve in the military. All employers must provide up to 16 hours of unpaid leave per school year so that parents or guardians can attend school conferences or activities otherwise scheduled during the work day. Employers with at least 20 employees are required to provide up to 40 hours paid leave for any employee donating bone marrow.

Whistleblower Statutes
Under Minnesota and federal law, an employer may not fire a worker in retaliation for reporting a violation of law or for refusing to participate in activity the employee believes to be illegal. If an employee acts in good faith and reports suspected illegal activities to the employer, any governmental agency or law enforcement officer, the employee cannot be fired or be treated adversely. The employee may, but need not, go through internal employer-sponsored channels to report suspected illegal activity.

Employee Access to Personnel Records
Employees who work for companies with 20 or more employees are guaranteed access to their personnel records. An employee is anyone currently working for the company or who has been separated for less than one year. Independent contractors are not covered.

The personnel record includes: application, wage or salary history, commendations, warnings, discharge or termination letters, employment history and job titles, and performance evaluations. In most situations, the personnel record does not include written references, information regarding allegations of criminal misconduct, results of employer administered tests or statements or portions of statements by coworkers concerning job performance that would disclose the identity of the coworker by name, inference or otherwise.

E M P L O Y M E N T   L A W :   I N D I V I D U A L

Reinhardt & Anderson
1000 E. First National Bank Building
332 Minnesota Street
St. Paul, MN 55101

Phone: (612) 227-9990
Fax: (612) 297-6543

JEFFREY R.
ANDERSON

JEFFREY R. ANDERSON: Mr. Anderson is a plaintiffs' trial lawyer and litigation specialist concentrating in sexual abuse, employment discrimination and professional malpractice. He has successfully litigated more than 200 jury trials to verdict and has gained a national reputation for representing victims of sexual abuse. Mr. Anderson is a tireless champion of civil rights representing the injured or displaced in a variety of cases, i.e., sexual, racial, age discrimination, whistleblowing, professional malpractice and sexual exploitation. He has presented more than 100 lectures on trial skills and represented plaintiffs in personal injury actions, and has authored more than a dozen publications and articles on topics of sexual abuse, professional malpractice and employment law. He is a partner in the St. Paul litigation law firm of Reinhardt & Anderson and is Board Certified as a Civil Trial Specialist by the National Board of Trial Advocacy and the Minnesota State Bar Association.

Education: JD 1975, William Mitchell; BA 1970 magna cum laude, University of Minnesota.

Admitted: 1975 Minnesota; 1977 U.S. Ct. App. (8th Cir.), 1980 U.S. Sup. Ct.; 1980 U.S. Ct. App. (9th Cir.); 1984 Wisconsin; 1984 U.S. Dist. Ct. (E. Dist. WI); 1984 U.S. Dist. Ct. (W. Dist. WI.).

Employment History: Partner/Attorney 1981-present, Reinhardt & Anderson; Attorney/Sole Practitioner 1975-81, Jeffrey R. Anderson, P.A.

Representative Clients: *Mrozka v. Archdiocese of St. Paul and Minneapolis,* sexual abuse by clergy; *Stanks v. Minnesota Police Recruitment System,* racial discrimination; *Gilshannon et. al., v. Archdiocese,* age discrimination.

Professional Associations: MTLA; Board of Professional Liability Attorneys; National Employment Lawyers Assn.; ATLA; Minnesota Employment Lawyers Assn.; NBTA; Trial Lawyers for Public Justice.

Community Involvement: Minnesota State Board of Public Defense 1994-present (Board Member—appointed by Minnesota Supreme Court); Rivertown Restoration Society; National Institute of Adolescent and Child Sexual Health (Board Member).

Firm: Reinhardt & Anderson is a 15-lawyer firm representing plaintiffs in personal injury and class action commercial litigation. The firm has developed a national reputation in class actions, employment discrimination and sexual abuse. The firm's office is located in St. Paul but it handles cases in more than 25 states across the country. *See complete firm profile in the Firm Profiles section.*

Employment Law: Individual

Don L. Bye, P.A.
2802 West First Street
Duluth, MN 55806

Phone: (218) 628-0940
Fax: (218) 628-0889

Don L. Bye

DON L. BYE: Mr. Bye has represented labor unions and individual employees for more than 33 years. He has substantial court experience in varied types of litigation, including accident and personal injury, products liability and business litigation. He is a speaker at legal seminars, an occasional lecturer at area colleges and has written several legal articles. Mr. Bye represents unions in all matters: NLRD and BMS representation and elections, grievance and arbitration, contract interpretation and bargaining, unfair labor practices, injunctive proceedings and court actions. He has been listed in *The Best Lawyers in America* since 1987.

Education: LLB 1963, University of Minnesota; BA 1963, University of Minnesota; AA 1955, Brainerd Community College.

Admitted: 1963 Minnesota; 1963 U.S. Dist. Ct. (MN); 1967 U.S. Claims Ct.

Employment History: Mr. Bye has been an attorney in Duluth for the past 34 years and is a former union carpenter.

Representative Clients: Mr. Bye's clients include Duluth and Iron Range building trades, ironworkers, electrical workers, laborers, plumbers, sheet metal workers, roofers, machinists and woodworkers; service unions (Hotel and Restaurant); Teamsters; public employees (AFSCME, SEIU); teachers (MFT and Duluth Federation of Teachers); communications workers; supervisory associations; law enforcement; and health care organizations.

Professional Associations: MSBA (Board of Governors 1988-91); ABA; National Employment Lawyers' Assn.; 11th District Bar Assn. (President 1988); University of Minnesota Industrial Relations Advisory Council; Board of Legal Certification 1987-93; Public Employment Relations Board 1972-81.

Community Involvement: Kids' Voting USA; Arrowhead Food Bank (Chair 1983-92); SHARE Food Drive (Chair or Cochair 1982-91); National Bone Marrow Donor Bank 1981-85; Duluth Planning Commission 1967-75.

Firm: Don L. Bye, P.A., concentrates in litigation and labor matters in public and private sectors. The firm also handles all types of employment disputes.

Extensive Experience In:
- Public Employment Law
- Arbitration & Mediation
- Veteran's Preference

EMPLOYMENT LAW: INDIVIDUAL

The Cooper Law Firm, Chartered
4747 First Bank Place
602 Second Avenue South
Minneapolis, MN 55402

Phone: (612) 332-9002
Fax: (612) 332-4903

STEPHEN W.
COOPER

STEPHEN W. COOPER: Mr. Cooper's practice focuses primarily on civil and human rights cases, including racial discrimination, sexual harassment, gender discrimination, age discrimination, disability discrimination, whistleblower violations, unjust termination and negligence. In the area of discrimination, Mr. Cooper handles employment, business, public accommodation, education, housing and other situations as well as other forms of civil litigation ranging from medical malpractice to personal injury. Mr. Cooper has taught classes or guest lectured at both the law school and the undergraduate level and at continuing legal education programs, many on human rights law. He has won several awards, including the 1989 Minnesota Access Achievement Award for Outstanding Government Distinguished Contribution and Achievement Towards Persons with Disabilities; the 1989 Leadership Award Supporting Affirmative Action for Persons with Disabilities; the Arizona Civil Liberties Union's 1986 Defense of Justice and Civil Liberties Award; and the ACLU of Southern California's 1986 Annual Commitment for Preserving Justice Award. In 1989 he was selected as one of the "Newsmakers for Women's Issues," by *Minnesota Women's Press* and in 1987 he was a finallst for "Trial Lawyer of the Year," by Trial Lawyers for Public Interest in Washington, D.C.
Education: JD 1976, Emory University; BA 1973, Case Western Reserve University.
Admitted: 1976 Minnesota; 1976 Georgia; 1976 U.S. Ct. App. (5th Cir.; 8th Cir.); 1980 U.S. Sup. Ct.
Employment History: Founding Member 1991-present, The Cooper Law Firm, Chartered; Commissioner 1987-91, Department of Human Rights; Executive Director 1978-87, Neighborhood Justice Center; Staff Attorney 1976-78, Neighborhood Justice Center; Law Clerk 1973-76, Federal Public Defender Program, Atlanta; Law Clerk, U.S. Justice Department, Antitrust Division, Regional Headquarters, Atlanta; Law Clerk, Weiner & Bazemore, Jonesboro, GA; Law Clerk, Dekalb County Sheriff's Department.
Representative Clients: Mr. Cooper was trial counsel in the Texas and Arizona sanctuary cases representing church workers who were prosecuted by the federal government for assisting Central American refugees. He represented Mark Baloga in his sexual harassment case against City Council Member Paula MacAbbee. Other clients include a dispatcher in her successful whistleblower case against Dakota County for retaliating against her for enforcing the no-smoking ban; a delivery service person in his case against an airline because employees masqueraded as Ku Klux Klan members; a police officer in his case of racial discrimination against the police department; and other cases of discrimination, unfair treatment or injury.
Professional Associations: ATLA; National Employment Lawyers' Assn.; MTLA; Metropolitan Center for Independent Living.

EMPLOYMENT LAW:INDIVIDUAL

Gregg M. Corwin & Associates
1660 South Highway 100
Suite 508 East
St. Louis Park, MN 55416-1534

Phone: (612) 544-7774
Fax: (612) 544-7151

GREGG M. CORWIN

GREGG M. CORWIN: Mr. Corwin has been practicing labor and employment law for almost 25 years. With special emphasis in union-side public sector law and discrimination law, he was instrumental in drafting the Minnesota Pay Equity Act, the amendments to the Minnesota Public Employment Labor Relations Act and the Minnesota Government Data Practices Act. Mr. Corwin is a popular seminar lecturer on union representation, public sector law, sexual harassment, the American Disabilities Act, defamation, discrimination, data privacy, arbitration and wrongful discharge. He appears in *The Best Lawyers in America* in all editions since 1989, as well as the 1993-97 issues of *Bar Register of Preeminent Lawyers* in the Labor/Employment Law area.
Education: JD 1972 cum laude, University of Minnesota; BA 1969 summa cum laude, University of Minnesota (Phi Beta Kappa).
Admitted: 1972 Minnesota; 1972 U.S. Dist. Ct. (MN); 1976 U.S. Ct. App. (8th Cir.); 1977 U.S. Sup. Ct.
Employment History: 1978-present, Gregg M. Corwin & Associates.
Representative Clients: American Federation of State, County and Municipal Employees Council Nos. 6 and 14; Minnesota Assn. of Professional Employees; Amalgamated Transit Union Local 1005; City Employees Union, Local 363 Laborers; International Assn. of Firefighters, Local 82; Minneapolis Police Federation; Hennepin County Sheriff's Deputy Assn.; Highway Patrol Supervisors Assn.
Professional Associations: AFL-CIO Lawyers Coordinating Committee (Charter Member 1982-present); HCBA [Labor and Employment Law Section (Treasurer 1988-89)]; MSBA (Governing Council); ABA; National Employment Lawyers Assn.
Firm: Gregg M. Corwin & Associates has established itself as a leader in Minnesota labor law by representing numerous public employee unions. The firm has participated in many first impression cases on an appellate basis that deal with Minnesota's Public Employment Labor Relations Act, the Minnesota Human Rights Act and the Minnesota Government Data Practices Act. In the past several years, the firm has expanded its employment law practice, representing both plaintiffs and defendants in sexual harassment and discrimination cases. The firm has obtained six-figure verdicts in two recent employment cases. In addition to Mr. Corwin's expertise, the firm's associate attorneys have established expertise in labor and employment law. Karin Peterson represents both plaintiffs and defendants in employment law cases and unions in grievances and litigation, and Nancy Ossenfort Booth represents law enforcement officers in employment matters.

Extensive Experience In:
• Public Sector Employment Law
• Data Practices Issues
• Arbitration & Mediation

E M P L O Y M E N T   L A W :   I N D I V I D U A L

Muir, Heuel, Carlson & Spelhaug, P.A.
404 Marquette Bank Building
P.O. Box 1057
Rochester, MN 55903
Phone: (507) 288-4110
Fax: (507) 288-4122
800: (800) 282-4110

DANIEL J. HEUEL

DANIEL J. HEUEL: Mr. Heuel engages in civil trial practice in federal and state courts throughout Minnesota principally representing injured persons and their families in a wide variety of claims involving personal injury, products liability, professional liability, contract disputes and business torts. He has a substantial subspecialty in employment law, wrongful discharge, civil rights violations, defamation and representing victims of sexual harassment in the workplace. To his credit, he obtained the highest jury verdict for damages ever returned in Olmsted County. Mr. Heuel was acknowledged as a "Super Lawyer" in 1995 and 1996 by *Minnesota Law & Politics.*

Education: JD 1978, University of Minnesota; BA 1974 summa cum laude, St. Mary's University.

Admitted: 1978 Minnesota; 1980 U.S. Ct. App. (8th Cir.).

Employment History: 1978-present, Muir, Heuel, Carlson & Spelhaug, P.A.; 1974-75, United States Department of Labor.

Representative Clients: Mr. Heuel represents persons wrongfully injured, including quadriplegics, amputees, and the physically and emotionally disabled. He also represents estates of spouses, parents and children for death by wrongful act.

Professional Associations: Third District Bar Assn. (past President 1993-94); MSBA (Certified Civil Trial Specialist); American Arbitration Assn. (Commercial Arbitrator).

Community Involvement: Mr. Heuel's interests include raising horses on his farm in rural Olmsted County, sailing, motorcycling, darkroom photography and playing amateur baseball in a local league.

Firm: Muir, Heuel, Carlson & Spelhaug, P.A., was founded in Rochester in 1966 by Ross Muir as a firm devoted exclusively to trial practice. Over the course of 30 years, the firm has grown in experience and reputation as an aggressive and ethical advocate for injured persons, always focusing on its area of specialty by resisting the urge to diversify into a general practice. The firm includes four partners, three of whom are Board Certified Civil Trial Specialists, with nearly 100 years of combined experience trying and settling some of the largest and most important civil cases in the area. Assisted by a staff that includes two certified legal investigators, the firm continues to stand up for the rights of the physically disabled, the estates of the wrongfully killed, and victims of civil rights violations, many of whom are referred from other lawyers and judges who have developed respect for the skills, energy, and creativity of Muir, Heuel, Carlson & Spelhaug, P.A. *See complete firm profile in the Firm Profiles section.*

Extensive Experience In:
• Sexual Harassment
• Discrimination
• Wrongful Discharge

EMPLOYMENT LAW: INDIVIDUAL

Horton and Associates
4930 West 77th Street
Suite 210
Minneapolis, MN 55435-4804

Phone: (612) 831-6900
Fax: (612) 893-3126
E-mail: horton@winternet.com
Web Site: www.hortonlaw.com

DONALD E.
HORTON

DONALD E. HORTON: An accomplished trial attorney, Mr. Horton has more than 22 years of experience in employment law. He has taught employment law courses as a member of the adjunct faculty at William Mitchell College of Law and the University of St. Thomas. He has litigated several high-profile cases including *Flower v. K-Mart* ($3.2 million jury award in a sexual harassment case). Mr. Horton has represented individuals and organizations in employment-related matters in 19 states, Europe and Japan. He has coauthored a book and all or part of 14 treatises on employment law, is a frequent presenter at employment law seminars and has been heard on National Public Radio's *All Things Considered.*
Education: JD 1974, William Mitchell; MA 1994, University of St. Thomas; BA 1970, University of St. Thomas.
Admitted: 1974 Minnesota; 1974 U.S. Dist. Ct. (MN); 1977 U.S. Ct. App. (8th Cir.); 1984 U.S. Ct. App. (Fed. Cir.).
Employment History: President 1985-present, Horton and Associates; Partner 1982-85, Horton and Langevin; Staff Labor Relations Attorney 1978-82, Northwest Airlines; Private Practice 1974-78.
Representative Clients: Mr. Horton represents persons who have experienced sexual harassment, discrimination and other types of unlawful employment actions.
Professional Associations: MSBA 1974-present (Labor and Employment Law Section 1974-present; Pro Bono Services Panel 1982-present); HCBA (Labor and Employment Law Section 1982-present).
Community Involvement: Operation Uplift 1989-present (Founder); St. Mark's Church 1994-present (Family Mediator).
Firm: Horton and Associates is recognized as a leading employment law firm. The firm practices exclusively in this area, with special emphasis on unemployment compensation, discrimination, sexual harassment, whistleblowing, retaliatory discharge, defamation and contract cases. Horton and Associates is committed to providing the highest quality legal services in the most ethical manner. *See complete firm profile in the Firm Profiles section.*

Extensive Experience In:
• Employment Discrimination
• Sexual Harassment
• Wrongful Discharge

E M P L O Y M E N T   L A W :   I N D I V I D U A L

Nichols Kaster & Anderson
4644 IDS Center
80 South Eighth Street
Minneapolis, MN 55402-2242

Phone: (612) 338-1919
Fax: (612) 338-4878
Web Site: www.nka.com

JAMES H. KASTER

JAMES H. KASTER: Mr. Kaster's primary emphasis is in trial practice. His extensive trial experience allows him to be a frequent lecturer and author of articles on trial and employment law issues. Mr. Kaster has appeared on the *CBS Evening News* and *Good Morning America* as a special guest on employee polygraph tests. He has litigated several high-profile cases including *Lundman v. McKown* ($14.2 million jury award in the first wrongful death lawsuit against the First Church of Christ, Scientist, where an 11-year-old boy died as a result of exclusive reliance on spiritual healing); *Zumberge v. Northern States Power Company* (stray voltage case resulting in a $1 million award); *Kamrath v. Suburban National Bank* (an emotional distress award was granted for taking and passing an employment lie detector test); *Lynch v. Dooley and Pomaville* (the "Viking Chevrolet" case, a $2.3 million verdict in a shareholder suit); and *Nordling v. Northern States Power* (established the right of in-house lawyers to sue for wrongful discharge in Minnesota).
Education: JD 1979, Marquette University; BA 1976 cum laude, Marquette University (Phi Beta Kappa).
Admitted: 1980 Minnesota.
Employment History: Partner 1984-present, Nichols Kaster & Anderson; Associate 1980-83, Nichols Kruger Starks & Carruthers.
Professional Associations: NDTA (Certified Civil Trial Specialist); MSBA [Criminal Law Section (past Chair)]; Academy of Certified Trial Lawyers of Minnesota; HCBA; Wisconsin State Bar Assn.; MTLA (Board of Governors); ATLA.
Community Involvement: Alpha Sigma Nu (National Jesuit Honor Society). *See complete firm profile in the Firm Profiles section.*

EMPLOYMENT LAW: INDIVIDUAL

GERALD T. LAURIE

Lapp, Laurie, Libra, Abramson & Thomson, Chartered
One Financial Plaza
Suite 1800
120 South Sixth Street
Minneapolis, MN 55402
Phone: (612) 338-5815
Fax: (612) 338-6651

GERALD T. LAURIE: Mr. Laurie, a Civil Trial Specialist Certified by the Minnesota State Bar Association, has more than 25 years of experience practicing law. He has practiced employment law for more than 10 years in the areas of discrimination (age, race, gender and disability), whistleblowing, sexual harassment, wrongful termination, executive severance packages, noncompete agreements, trade secrets and other commercial litigation. Mr. Laurie argued one of the state's leading cases in employment law and has obtained large jury verdicts, including one of $1,200,000 for an employee, and another of $3,250,000 in which two former employees of his client's small company copied its products, violating patent and trademark laws. He has represented many clients in substantial sexual harassment settlements. Mr. Laurie is a frequent lecturer and writer on employment law. His articles include: "Non-Compete Agreements: Are They Valid?" <I>*Minnesota Business Journal,* July 1983; Coauthor, "The Latest Look at Wrongful Termination," *Minnesota Trial Lawyer,* 1985 Vol. 10 No. 2 p. 6; Coauthor "Court Rules That Employment Discrimination Claims Survive the Claimants Death," *Minnesota Trial Lawyers,* Spring 1990.

Education: JD 1967, University of Minnesota (Minnesota Law Review 1966-67); BA 1964 cum laude, University of Minnesota.

Admitted: 1967 Minnesota; 1967 U.S. Dist. Ct. (MN); 1970 U.S. Tax Ct.; 1971 U.S. Ct. App. (8th Cir.); 1987 U.S. Ct. App. (Fed. Cir.).

Employment History: Founder/Shareholder 1970-present, Lapp, Laurie, Libra, Abramson & Thomson, Chartered; Special Assistant Attorney General 1968-69, Minnesota Department of Revenue.

Representative Clients: Mr. Laurie represents employees, executives, individuals, sexual harassment victims and small to medium-sized companies.

Professional Associations: HCBA [Community Relations Committee (Chair 1973-74)]; MSBA; ABA; ATLA; MTLA [Commercial Litigation Section (Cochair 1979-85; Board of Governors 1981-88)]; National Employment Lawyers Assn.; Academy of Certified Trial Lawyers of Minnesota; American College of Labor and Employment Lawyers (Fellow).

Firm: With 13 lawyers, Lapp, Laurie, Libra, Abramson & Thomson, Chartered, is also involved in business and corporate tax law, commercial litigation, real estate law, commercial leases, tax planning and representation, financial reorganization, bankruptcy, securities, personal injury, medical malpractice and wrongful death, retirement planning, estate planning and administration, and family law. *See complete firm profile in the Firm Profiles section.*

Extensive Experience In:
• Executive Termination
• Noncompetes
• Discrimination

EMPLOYMENT LAW: INDIVIDUAL

William J. Mavity & Associates
2525 Metropolitan Centre
333 South Seventh Street
Minneapolis, MN 55402

Phone: (612) 339-3001
Fax: (612) 339-3267

WILLIAM J.
MAVITY

WILLIAM J. MAVITY: As a Minnesota State Bar Association Certified Civil Trial Specialist, Mr. Mavity represents plaintiffs in matters relating to sexual harassment, sexual and racial discrimination, employment law, medical malpractice, products liability and other personal injury civil litigation. He served as a hearing examiner in Minnesota's United States District Court for the class action Consent Decree claims process in *Aribume, et al. v. Northwest Airlines, Inc.,* 1992-96. Mr. Mavity has written and lectured extensively on sexual harassment and employment law. His lectures include "The Cheryl Turner Case," presented to the Hennepin County Bar Association Labor/Employment Committee in September 1991 and "Basic Employment Discrimination Law," presented at the Minnesota Institute of Legal Education's Employment Seminar. He is the author of "The Evaluation of a Sexual Harassment Claim," *Harassment in the Workplace,* MILE, March 1992. In 1991, he obtained the largest settlement at the time in a sexual harassment case against the State of Minnesota (*Cheryl Turner v. Minnesota State Patrol, et al.*).
Education: JD 1982, University of Minnesota; BA 1979, University of Minnesota
Admitted: 1982 Minnesota; 1983 U.S. Ct. App. (8th Cir.); 1988 U.S. Sup. Ct.; 1992 U.S. Dist. Ct. (W. Dist. TX), 1992 Wisconsin; 1993 U.S. Dist. Ct. (MN).
Professional Associations: HCBA; RCBA; MSBA; Wisconsin State Bar Assn.; Federal Bar Assn.; ABA; National Employment Lawyers Assn.; Academy of Certified Trial Lawyers of Minnesota; Minnesota Institute of Legal Education Employment Seminars (Faculty).

SUSAN A. MCKAY

McKay Law Office
305 America Avenue
Bemidji, MN 56601
Phone: (218) 759-9688
Fax: (218) 759-9692
800: (800) 640-9688
E-mail: smckay@mail.paulbunyan.net

SUSAN A. MC KAY: Ms. McKay practices primarily in employment, family and criminal law. She has successfully represented individual clients in discrimination, public employment and criminal issues and family matters involving contested custody.

Education: JD 1987, University of North Dakota; BA 1984 summa cum laude, Moorhead State University.

Admitted: 1989 Minnesota; 1987 North Dakota; 1990 U.S. Dist. Ct. (MN); 1996 U.S. Ct. App. (8th Cir.).

Employment History: Owner 1995-present, McKay Law Office; Associate 1989-95, McRae & McRae, P.A.; Clerk 1987-89, Ninth Judicial District.

Representative Clients: Plaintiffs' discrimination and public employees.

Professional Associations: National Employment Lawyers Assn. 1992-present; ABA 1987-present; Beltrami County Bar Assn. 1989-present; MSBA 1989-present.

Community Involvement: Upper Mississippi Mental Health Center (Cochair); Northwoods Coalition for Battered Women (Cochair).

Firm: Founded in 1995, McKay Law Office represents employment clients in northern Minnesota and other areas throughout the state. Ms. McKay has previous experience in personnel service and government employment. The firm also provides representation in family and criminal matters.

Extensive Experience In:
- Discrimination
- Public Employment
- Custody

EMPLOYMENT LAW: INDIVIDUAL

Miller • O'Brien • Bloom
1208 Plymouth Building
12 South Sixth Street
Minneapolis, MN 55402-1529

Phone: (612) 333-5831
Fax: (612) 342-2613
800: (800) 850-8335
E-mail: nmiller@m-o-b.com

NANCY MILLER

NANCY MILLER: Ms. Miller devotes her practice entirely to employment and labor law. While she has successfully represented individuals at trial and at contested civil service and unemployment hearings, she also has substantial experience resolving employee rights claims through alternative dispute resolution procedures, such as mediation.

Education: JD 1989, Northeastern University; BA 1986, College of St. Catherine.

Admitted: 1989 Minnesota; 1989 U.S. Dist. Ct (MN); 1996 U.S. Dist. Ct. (W. Dist. WI).

Employment History: Associate 1993-present, Miller • O'Brien • Bloom; Associate 1989-93, Gray, Plant, Mooty, Mooty & Bennett.

Representative Clients: Ms. Miller represents executive, middle manager and hourly employees in claims against employers for discrimination, breach of contract, retaliation and other common law and statutory causes of action.

Professional Associations: MTLA; National Employment Lawyers Assn.; MSBA.

Community Involvement: Ms. Miller is a former volunteer worker for legal advice clinics providing pro bono representation.

Firm: The firm's lawyers are widely known for representing employees and labor organizations in all types of employment and labor disputes and for their expertise in workers' compensation and personal injury. Founding partner Richard A. Miller is listed in *The Best Lawyers in America* for his labor and employment expertise. Founding Partner Maurice W. "Bill" O'Brien is recognized by his peers as a preeminent employment attorney handling all types of employment disputes. Michael Bloom heads the firm's workers' compensation practice and practices in union-side labor and employment law with a special emphasis on disability discrimination. Partner Daniel Froehlich is responsible for the firm's personal injury practice and also handles employment-related disputes. Nancy Miller practices primarily in labor and employment law. Miller • O'Brien • Bloom is committed to providing its clients with superior legal representation including a strong commitment to alternative dispute resolution. *See complete firm profile in the Firm Profiles section.*

Extensive Experience In:
• Discrimination
• Retaliation Cases

EMPLOYMENT LAW: INDIVIDUAL

Reinhardt & Anderson
1000 E. First National Bank Building
332 Minnesota Street
St. Paul, MN 55101

Phone: (612) 227-9990
Fax: (612) 297-6543

JOANNE JIRIK
MULLEN

JOANNE JIRIK MULLEN: Ms. Mullen is a plaintiffs' trial lawyer concentrating in employment discrimination, personal injury and wrongful death. She has represented employees on a variety of issues, including sexual, racial, age and disability discrimination claims. During the course of her practice, Ms. Mullen has been involved in all aspects of the litigation and appellate process and has tried several jury trials. Ms. Mullen has been recognized as a Leading Minnesota Attorney in the area of employment law.

Education: JD 1988, William Mitchell; BA 1983, College of St. Catherine's.

Admitted: 1988 Minnesota; 1989 U.S. Dist. Ct. (MN); 1989 U.S. Ct. App. (8th Cir.).

Employment History: Ms. Mullen is a partner who has practiced with Reinhardt & Anderson since her graduation from William Mitchell College of Law in 1988.

Representative Clients: Ms. Mullen has represented St. Paul Black Fire Fighters, plaintiffs in the Stroh Brewery litigation and numerous other plaintiffs against many Minnesota and national employers.

Professional Associations: National Employment Lawyers Assn. [Minnesota Chapter (Secretary/Treasurer)]; MTLA [Employment Committee (Cochair); Board of Governors]; ABA; MSBA; RCBA (Diversity Committee).

Community Involvement: Ms. Mullen is past president of the Friends of the St. Paul Chamber Orchestra; a volunteer at the College of St. Catherine's; a President's Forum member and volunteers with the St. Paul Chamber Orchestra and other arts organizations.

Firm: Reinhardt & Anderson is a 15-lawyer firm representing plaintiffs in personal injury and class action commercial litigation. The firm has developed a national reputation in class action, employment discrimination and sexual abuse. The firm's office is located in St. Paul but it handles cases in more than 25 states nationwide. *See complete firm profile in the Firm Profiles section.*

EMPLOYMENT LAW: INDIVIDUAL

Nichols Kaster & Anderson
4644 IDS Center
80 South Eighth Street
Minneapolis, MN 55402-2242

Phone: (612) 338-1919
Fax: (612) 338-4878
Web Site: www.nka.com

DONALD H.
NICHOLS

DONALD H. NICHOLS: Mr. Nichols' devotes his practice exclusively to trial work. After graduating from law school in 1971, Mr. Nichols was selected to teach and assist students at the University of Minnesota. During this time, he handled hundreds of cases and obtained an early exposure to the courtroom. Within a few years he wrote his first legal publication and began lecturing to other lawyers and judges on many different aspects of trial practice. Each year, he lectures to several hundred lawyers and judges about various aspects of trial practice. As a result, he has become respected in many aspects of trial practice. Not only have several lawyers sought his advice on behalf of their own clients, but many lawyers have retained him on a personal basis. One of the greatest compliments a lawyer can receive is to be asked to represent another lawyer who is in a difficult situation; this confidence has been frequently bestowed upon Mr. Nichols. In more than 20 years of trial work, he has tried many well-known cases, some that have been landmark cases in criminal and civil law. One of the first cases to establish an executive's right to leave an employer and work for a competitor was such a case.

Education: JD 1971, University of Minnesota (*Law Review*); BS 1961, Augsburg College.

Admitted: 1971 Minnesota; 1973 U.S. Dist Ct (MN); 1976 U.S. Ct. App. (8th Cir.); 1979 U.S. Sup. Ct.

Employment History: Founding Partner 1974-present, Nichols Kaster & Anderson.

Professional Associations: National Employment Lawyers Assn.; ATLA; MTLA. *See complete firm profile in the Firm Profiles section.*.

EMPLOYMENT LAW: INDIVIDUAL

Miller • O'Brien • Bloom
1208 Plymouth Building
12 South Sixth Street
Minneapolis, MN 55402-1529

Phone: (612) 333-5831
Fax: (612) 342-2613

MAURICE W.
"BILL" O'BRIEN

MAURICE W. (BILL) O'BRIEN: Mr. O'Brien practices exclusively in labor and employment law. He has substantial experience in trial work and nonlitigation counseling and strategic positioning with clients concerning workplace disputes, wrongful termination, employment agreements, noncompete agreements and stock option agreements. Mr. O'Brien's representation often involves legal claims for wrongful termination; whistleblower violations; age, disability, sexual and racial discrimination; and sexual harassment. He also represents both building trades and nonbuilding trades unions in collective bargaining negotiations, arbitrations and unfair labor practice and representation cases before the National Labor Relations Board. He also has substantial agency experience with the Equal Employment Opportunity Commission, the Minnesota Department of Human Rights and the Department of Labor. Mr. O'Brien has a strong commitment to alternative dispute resolution. In 1994, he completed the Certified Minnesota General Mediation Training. He is a frequent speaker on labor and employment law topics.
Education: JD 1981, Northwestern University; BA 1977, Colgate University.
Admitted: 1981 Minnesota; 1981 U.S. Dist. Ct. (MN); 1981 U.S. Ct. App. (8th Cir.).
Employment History: Founding Partner 1985-present, Miller • O'Brien • Bloom; Associate 1981-85, Robins, Kaplan, Miller & Ciresi L.L.P.; Law Clerk 1980, Robins, Kaplan, Miller & Ciresi L.L.P. (formerly Robins, Davis & Lyons); Law Clerk 1980, Legal Aid Foundation, Chicago.
Representative Clients: Mr. O'Brien represents executives, middle managers, hourly employees, and employee groups and classes.
Professional Associations: MSBA [Labor and Employment Law Section (Chair 1989)]; ABA (Labor and Employment Section); National Employment Lawyers Association [Minnesota Chapter (President 1992-92, 1993-94)]; AFL-CIO Lawyer's Coordinating Committee.
Community Involvement: ACT, Inc.—disability rights advocates (past Volunteer Attorney); Volunteer Mediator.
Firm: The firm's lawyers are widely known for representating employees and labor organizations in all types of employment and labor disputes and for their expertise in workers' compensation and personal injury law. Founding partner Richard A. Miller is listed in *The Best Lawyers in America* for his labor and employment expertise. Founding partner Maurice W. "Bill" O'Brien is recognized by his peers as a preeminent employment attorney handling all types of employment disputes. Mr. Bloom heads the firm's workers' compensation practice and practices in union-side labor and employment law with a special emphasis on disability discrimination. Partner Daniel Froehlich is responsible for the firm's personal injury practice and also handles employment-related disputes. Nancy Miller practices primarily in labor and employment law. Miller • O'Brien • Bloom is committed to providing its clients with superior legal representation including a strong commitment to alternative dispute resolution. *See complete firm profile in the Firm Profiles section.*

Extensive Experience In:
- Discrimination
- Sexual Harassment
- Wrongful Termination

EMPLOYMENT LAW: INDIVIDUAL

Attorney at Law
3908 IDS Center
80 South Eighth Street
Minneapolis, MN 55402

Phone: (612) 630-0010
Fax: (612) 630-0015

JAMES G. RYAN

JAMES G. RYAN: Mr. Ryan has been practicing employment law since 1984, and handles cases dealing with sexual harassment, discrimination (sexual, age, racial and disability), employment contracts, defamation, noncompetition agreements, trade secret disputes and other employment-related claims. In addition, he handles cases involving medical malpractice, products liability and personal injury. Mr. Ryan also represents the principals in disputes between business partners and shareholders in close corporations. He has written and lectured extensively on civil litigation, sexual harassment, discrimination and defamation. He has extensive civil appellate experience, having handled many appeals and authored more than 100 appellate briefs in the course of his career. In 1991, after a seven-day trial in *Vovk v. Tom Thumb Food Markets, Inc.*, he obtained a substantial award of damages in the only known decision in which a supervisor has prevailed against an employer for sexual harassment by a subordinate.

Education: JD 1978, University of Wisconsin; 1979-83, University of Minnesota Philosophy PhD Program; BA 1975, University of Wisconsin-Madison.

Admitted: 1984 Minnesota, 1978 Wisconsin; 1978 U.S. Dist. Ct. (W. Dist. WI); 1984 U.S. Dist. Ct. (MN); 1987 U.S. Ct. App. (8th Cir.).

Employment History: Sole Practitioner 1997-present; Partner 1984-97, Mavity & Ryan.

Professional Associations: National Employment Lawyers Assn.; MSBA; Wisconsin State Bar Assn.; ATLA; MTLA; HCBA; RCBA.

Extensive Experience In:
• Sexual Harassment
• Discrimination
• Defamation

EMPLOYMENT LAW: INDIVIDUAL

Winthrop & Weinstine, P.A.
3200 Minnesota World Trade Center
30 East Seventh Street
St. Paul, MN 55101

Phone: (612) 290-8400
Fax: (612) 292-9347

STEPHEN J. SNYDER

STEPHEN J. SNYDER: Mr. Snyder handles a full spectrum of employment law matters. He has represented many individuals in multiparty, classwide claims arising from discrimination in the workplace. Mr. Snyder is best known for his work on behalf of employees terminated due to age discrimination. Since 1992, he has served as lead counsel for the plaintiffs in three well-known employment law class actions against IDS Financial Services, Svedala Industries, Monsanto Company and Chevron Chemical Company that collectively resulted in settlements for the plaintiffs for more than $57 million. Mr. Snyder is also a frequent lecturer to attorneys as part of the Minnesota Continuing Legal Education program.

Education: JD 1972 cum laude, Harvard University; BS Physics 1969 with high distinction, University of Minnesota (Phi Beta Kappa).

Admitted: 1972 Minnesota; 1976 U.S. Dist. Ct. (MN); 1977 U.S. Sup. Ct.; 1980 U.S. Ct. App. (8th Cir.).

Employment History: Shareholder 1986-present, Winthrop & Weinstine, P.A.; Associate/Partner 1972, 1976-85, Gray, Plant, Mooty, Mooty & Bennett, P.A.; Attorney 1973-75, United States Navy Judge Advocate General's Corps.

Professional Associations: ABA (Labor Law Section; Employment Law Section); MSBA; HCBA.

Community Involvement: Minnesota Center for Environmental Advocacy (Board Member).

Extensive Experience In:
- Age Discrimination
- Class Actions

EMPLOYMENT LAW: INDIVIDUAL

Mansfield & Tanick, P.A.
1560 International Centre
900 Second Avenue South
Minneapolis, MN 55402-3383

Phone: (612) 339-4295
Fax: (612) 339-3161
E-mail: tanick@mansfieldtanick.com
Web Site: www.mansfieldtanick.com

MARSHALL H.
TANICK

MARSHALL H. TANICK: Mr. Tanick is Certified as a Civil Trial Specialist by the Minnesota State Bar Association with special emphasis on representation of individuals and business organizations in connection with employment law, defamation and media law, constitutional law and other matters. He has represented many individuals and companies in dealing with resolution of workplace disputes, including contract negotiations, labor-management matters, discrimination, sexual harassment and wrongful termination. He helped pioneer the structuring of severance arrangements on a nontaxable basis for benefit of business and individual clients. Mr. Tanick has written several dozen publications concerning a variety of constitutional and employment law issues, including "Contesting Constitutional Cases," *Hennepin Lawyer.*
Education: JD 1973, Stanford University (Order of the Coif); BA 1969, University of Minnesota.
Admitted: 1974 Minnesota; 1974 California; 1974 U.S. Dist. Ct. (MN); 1974 U.S. Ct. App. (8th Cir.); 1990 U.S. Sup. Ct.; 1992 U.S. Ct. App. (3rd Cir.).
Employment History: Partner 1989-present, Mansfield & Tanick, P.A.; Attorney 1976-89, Tanick & Heins; Attorney 1974-76, Robins, Davis & Lyons; Law Clerk 1973-74, Honorable Earl R. Larson, United States District Court, District of Minnesota.
Professional Associations: ABA [*Litigation* (Editor)]; MSBA; HCBA [*Hennepin Lawyer* (Editor)]; American Arbitration Assn.
Community Involvement: Minnesota News Council; University of Minnesota Alumni Assn.; American Dog Owners Assn.
Firm: Mansfield & Tanick, P.A., is a full-service law firm with emphasis on civil litigation, employment and workplace matters, discrimination and harassment, including defamation, privacy, media law and other matters. The firm also represents business and nonprofit organizations dealing with commercial issues, partnership and shareholder disputes, and other legal matters. Mansfield & Tanick, P.A., is committed to finding legal solutions for its clients through superior competence, hard work, responsiveness and dedicated advocacy. *See complete firm profile in the Firm Profiles section.*

Extensive Experience In:
* Defamation, Libel & Slander
* Noncompete Agreements
* Sexual Harassment/Discrimination

EMPLOYMENT LAW: INDIVIDUAL

Philip G. Villaume & Associates
7900 International Drive
Suite 675
Bloomington, MN 55425

Phone: (612) 851-0823
Fax: (612) 851-0824

PHILIP G.
VILLAUME

PHILIP G. VILLAUME: Mr. Villaume concentrates his practice in employment law, representing professionals facing employment-related misconduct allegations. He represents victims of workplace abuse and harassment. Mr. Villaume has represented more than 500 professionals since 1986, including 400 educators. He conducts workshops throughout the country on the prevention of workplace violence and harassment and is considered a national expert and consultant on topics of professional misconduct, harassment and violence in schools and in the workplace. Mr. Villaume was awarded a Certificate of Excellence in 1990 from Hamline University School of Law and the Judges Choice Award, Most Well-Prepared Lawyer in 1991. He has lectured for the National Institute for Trial Advocacy. He is an adjunct professor for the University of Minnesota and University of St. Thomas and is the Course Chair and lecturer on criminal law, trial skills and employment law for Minnesota Continuing Legal Education. He is the author of *The Law & Procedure Handbook for Minnesota Educators,* 1990; *The Better Work Environment,* 1997; and a coauthor of *Teachers At Risk,* 1993.
Education: JD 1979, Hamline University; BA 1971 magna cum laude, Macalester College.
Admitted: 1979 Minnesota; 1984 Wisconsin; 1984 U.S. Sup. Ct.
Employment History: 1979-present, Philip G. Villaume and Associates; Legal Investigator 1977-79, Villaume Investigative Services; Probation Officer 1972-76, Ramsey County Department of Community Corrections.
Representative Clients: Mr. Villaume represents educators, law enforcement officers, clergy, lawyers, physicians and other health care providers, business executives, corporations, educational institutions, professional associations and labor organizations including the Minnesota Police and Peace Officers Association and the Minnesota Federation of Teachers.
Professional Associations: MSBA; HCBA.
Firm: Founded in 1979, Philip G. Villaume and Associates has been providing legal services to professionals and organizations for the past 18 years. Mr. Villaume is a national leader in representing professionals accused of employment-related misconduct. He and his two associates have handled several of Minnesota's high-profile cases involving allegations of professional misconduct since 1985. In 1986, the law firm successfully defended the leading teacher rights case in the country, *State v. Gruhl;* and in 1990, a precedent-setting case before the Supreme Court involving religious freedom with respect to the Amish and the slow-moving vehicle emblem, *State v. Hershberger.* The firm also provides pro bono legal service to the Amish communities in Minnesota and Wisconsin. In 1996, the firm successfully handled the precedent-setting case, *York v. Wood,* that involved workplace harassment of a public school teacher by a parent.

EMPLOYMENT LAW: INDIVIDUAL

Messerli & Kramer, P.A.
150 South Fifth Street
Suite 1800
Minneapolis, MN 55402

Phone: (612) 672-3668
Fax: (612) 672-3777

JAMES C. WICKA

JAMES C. WICKA: Mr. Wicka represents employees who have been unfairly discriminated against, sexually harassed or forced to keep silent about illegal business activities. He is also known for his experience representing victims of serious accidents. Frequently, client suits are brought against Fortune 500 corporations and insurance companies. Mr. Wicka has worked on several high-profile cases and has developed and applied new theories of liability to compensate victims. He has appeared before the Minnesota Supreme Court three times and has taken many cases to trial. Jury verdicts for clients have reached six and seven figures.

Education: JD 1985, William Mitchell; BS 1981, University of Minnesota.

Admitted: 1985 Minnesota.

Employment History: Partner/Personal Litigation Practice Group Leader 1985-present, Messerli & Kramer, P.A.

Community Involvement: Pro bono work for Mothers Against Drunk Driving (MADD).

Professional Associations: ATLA; MTLA, MSBA.

Firm: Mr. Wicka is a partner and the Personal Litigation Practice Group Leader at Messerli and Kramer, P.A. The practice group includes attorneys Susan Coler, Jeff Ellis, Leanne Litfin and Steve Smith, all of whom are experienced representing individuals in complex cases. Additional support is provided by an in-house private investigator, seven-person support staff and the 40-plus attorneys at Messerli & Kramer, P.A. *See complete firm profile in the Firm Profiles section.*

Extensive Experience In:
• Whistleblowers
• Discrimination
• Sexual Harassment

HORTON AND ASSOCIATES
4930 West 77th Street, Suite 210 - Minneapolis, MN 55435-4804
Phone: (612) 831-6900, Fax: (612) 893-3126,
E-mail: horton@winternet.com, Web Site: www.hortonlaw.com

Don Horton   *David R. Kett*   *William A. Celebrezze*
      Michelle M. Lore   *Chrisine L. Kelly*

Horton and Associates is an employment law firm committed to providing the highest quality legal services in the most ethical manner. The firm handles matters that arise in an employment setting, with special emphasis on unemployment compensation, discrimination, sexual harassment, "whistleblowing," retaliatory discharge, defamation and contract cases.

Horton and Associates prides itself on its reputation for excellence and is pleased that many experienced lawyers and judges have referred their friends, neighbors and family members to the firm.

The firm's attorneys are well known within the legal community as outstanding employment lawyers. Firm members have taught courses and seminars on employment law topics, have served on various bar association employment-related committees and task forces, and have published related books and articles. **Donald Horton** has litigated several high-profile cases including *Flower v. K-Mart* ($3.2 million jury award in a sexual harassment case).

Horton and Associates believes communication with its clients is critical. A copy of all correspondence regarding a client's case is automatically sent to the client, and phone calls are returned promptly.

Horton and Associates knows that its clients value their privacy and does not invite public attention to its cases nor expose clients to press conferences.

Every employee of Horton and Associates has a desk sign that reads, "Are you looking for a solution, or are you in love with the problem?" It's a constant reminder that the firm's corporate philosophy is to look for solutions.

Horton and Associates' offices are conveniently located on the northeast corner of West 77th Street and Highway 100, just north of I-494. There is free parking right outside the door.

Visit the firm's Web Site for more information, or call FAXHELP at 893-3107 from the hand receiver of your fax machine and follow the prompts.

LAPP, LAURIE, LIBRA, ABRAMSON & THOMSON, CHARTERED

One Financial Plaza, Suite 1800 - 120 South Sixth Street - Minneapolis, MN 55402
Phone: (612) 338-5815, Fax: (612) 338-6651

Lapp, Laurie, Libra, Abramson & Thomson, Chartered, provides thoughtful and careful solutions for clients in various areas of business. The firm consists of 13 attorneys and staff members. Its primary resource is people—lawyers and staff who are dedicated to excellent, timely and economic client service. The firm strives to establish businesslike, friendly and long-term client relationships and to represent individuals and businesses in local, regional, national and international matters. It is committed to excellence in representing its clients by providing them legal services in the following areas:

• Business and Corporate Law
• Commercial Litigation
• Employment Law
• Civil Rights
• Real Estate Law
• Commercial Leases, Tax Planning and Representation
• Financial Reorganization and Bankruptcy
• Securities
• Personal Injury
• Medical Malpractice and Wrongful Death
• Retirement Planning
• Estate Planning and Administration
• Family Law

William S. Lapp is a founding member of the firm and the key person in the corporate, securities, business law and taxation areas. Mr. Lapp has substantial experience in negotiating complex business transactions but also spends a significant portion of his time advising individuals and businesses on the many legal issues they face. He is also experienced in securities litigation and arbitration. Mr. Lapp's background, tremendous negotiating skills, legal ability and desire to get the job done make him a valuable resource for businesses and individuals. From 1983-85, he served as Executive Committee Chair of the Hennepin County Bar Association's Securities Section.

Gerald T. Laurie was a founding member of the firm in 1970. His practice centers on employment and commercial litigation. He also serves as a mediator and is Certified as a Civil Trial Specialist by the Minnesota State Bar Association's Civil Trial Certification Council. Mr. Laurie has argued numerous cases before the Minnesota Supreme Court, is the author of legal articles and has lectured at legal education seminars on trade secret litigation, legal malpractice, sexual harassment, noncompete agreements and whistleblowing.

David A. Libra practices in real estate law and business law. He represents businesses and individuals in commercial and residential real estate purchases, financing and leasing. He also has substantial experience in organizing businesses, commercial contracts and estate planning for business owners. Mr. Libra is Certified as a Real Property Law Specialist by the Minnesota State Bar Association's Real Property Section and is a member of the Real Property Sections of the Minnesota State Bar Association and American Bar Association. He has been with the firm since 1973.

Frank Abramson focuses on family law, personal injury and sexual harassment/employment law. Mr. Abramson has 24 years of experience and has been active as an arbitrator and mediator in all types of legal disputes. His accounting degree from the University of Minnesota provides him with the background to analyze and evaluate the economic issues in divorce and the damage aspects of other areas of litigation.

Richard T. Thomson practices in business and employment litigation, including real estate, corporate, banking and bankruptcy litigation. He also serves as a mediator. His trial court, administrative and appellate victories include: *Eklund v. Vincent Brass,* one of the most significant wrongful termination cases in Minnesota; *TCF Mortgage Corp. v. Verex Assurance, Inc.,* the leading case in Minnesota on mortgage insurance law; *Berquist v. Anderson-Greenwood Aviation Corp.,* a major bankruptcy case; and *Ohio Calculating v. CPT Corp.,* an important case covering the rights of distributorships and manufacturers. He is a member of the American Bar Association and Minnesota State Bar Association and has published articles in legal periodicals concerning employment law and bankruptcy law.

MANSFIELD & TANICK, P.A.
1560 International Centre - 900 Second Avenue South
Minneapolis, MN 55402-3383
Phone: (612) 339-4295, Fax: (612) 339-3161
Web Site: www.mansfieldtanick.com

Mansfield & Tanick, P.A., is a rapidly growing law firm in downtown Minneapolis. Its practice extends throughout the Twin Cities community and greater Minnesota, the surrounding upper Midwest and nationwide in certain specialized litigation areas. The firm provides a full range of services, with special emphasis in business litigation and alternative dispute resolution (ADR), employment law, general business and commercial transaction practice, civil litigation, creditor-debtor relationships, media/defamation law, real estate law, estate and tax planning, financial reorganization, intellectual property and bankruptcy.

The firm's clients include high technology companies, newspapers, banks and consumer service companies such as American Harvest; Home Farmers Mutual Insurance Association; GME Consultants, Inc.; Minnesota Orthopedics, P.A.; Motel 6; Possis Medical, Inc.; Tremendous Productions; Reliable Automotive Corp.; and Resource Bank & Trust Company.

Employment Law. The firm provides a broad spectrum of legal advice to businesses and individuals relating to workplace issues; for example, in connection with discrimination, harassment, wrongful termination claims, employment contracts, severance arrangements, defamation and privacy matters, noncompete and other restrictive covenants, and management-labor relations.

Civil Litigation. The firm has extensive experience in litigation and ADR in commercial and business litigation, business fraud, breach of business contracts, shareholders and partners' business disputes, employment law, securities, media and defamation law, RICO, class action and other complex litigation.

Business Disputes. The firm frequently represents smaller companies in disputes with very large corporations. The firm's ADR department resolves legal disputes through alternative means, such as innovative prelitigation negotiations, arbitration and mediation, which frequently are quicker and less costly than conventional litigation.

General Corporate. The firm also provides a broad range of nonlitigation services, including representation of businesses in general corporate matters, commercial transactions, financial reorganization and bankruptcy, and representation of individuals in estate and tax planning.

The firm has seven partners, including Marshall H. Tanick and Seymour J. Mansfield (both of whom have been selected as Leading Minnesota Attorneys), Earl H. Cohen, Robert A. Johnson, Teresa Ayling, Richard Fuller and Sholly Blustin. The partners have a combined legal practice experience of more than 145 years and are backed-up by a very competent legal staff of six associate attorneys, a number of paralegals, law clerks and other professional staff. All lawyers are licensed in Minnesota and some are licensed in Illinois, Wisconsin, California and the District of Columbia. The firm's lawyers have outstanding academic and professional credentials and are committed to finding effective legal solutions for their clients through superior competence, hard work, responsiveness and dedicated advocacy.

MESSERLI & KRAMER, P.A.

150 South Fifth Street - Suite 1800 - Minneapolis, MN 55402
Phone: (612) 672-3600, Fax: (612) 672-3777

                    Susan Coler   *Jeff Ellis*
     Steve Smith   *Jim Wicka*   *Leanne Litfin*

Messerli & Kramer, P.A.'s Personal Litigation Practice Group represents employees who have been unfairly discriminated against, sexually harassed or forced to keep silent about illegal business activities. Additionally, the group represents people who have been injured by individuals, corporations or defective products. Leading Minnesota Attorney **Jim Wicka** is the practice group's chair.

In addition to Mr. Wicka, the group includes attorneys **Susan Coler, Jeff Ellis, Leanne Litfin** and **Steve Smith.** The depth and diversity of experience within this group provides clients with innovative and thorough legal representation. Additional support is given by an in-house private investigator, a seven-person support staff, and the 40-plus attorneys at Messerli & Kramer, P.A.

Mr. Wicka has worked on several high-profile cases and has developed and applied new theories of liability to compensate victims. He has appeared before the Minnesota Supreme Court three times and has taken many cases to trial. Jury verdicts for clients have reached six and seven figures.

The Personal Litigation Practice Group frequently represents clients in lawsuits against Fortune 500 corporations and insurance companies. The group's experience with employment and personal injury matters combined with the backing of Messerli & Kramer, P.A., provides a strong foundation for clients.

MILLER • O'BRIEN • BLOOM
1208 Plymouth Building - 12 South Sixth Street
Minneapolis, MN 55402-1529
Phone: (612) 333-5831, Fax: (612) 342-2613,

The firm's lawyers are widely known for representing employees and labor organizations in all types of employment and labor disputes and for their expertise in workers' compensation and personal injury. Founding partner Richard A. Miller is listed in *The Best Lawyers in America* for his labor and employment expertise; founding partner Maurice W. "Bill" O'Brien is recognized by his peers as a preeminent employment attorney handling all types of employment disputes; Michael Bloom heads the firm's workers' compensation practice and practices in union-side labor and employment law with a special emphasis on disability discrimination and wrongful termination; partner Daniel Froehlich is responsible for the firm's personal injury practice and handles labor and employment-related disputes; and Nancy Miller practices primarily in labor and employment law. Miller • O'Brien • Bloom is committed to providing its clients with superior legal representation, including a strong commitment to alternative dispute resolution.

Nancy Miller devotes her practice entirely to employment and labor law. While she has successfully represented individuals at trial and at contested civil service and unemployment hearings, she also has substantial experience resolving employee rights claims through alternative dispute resolution procedures, such as mediation.

Maurice W. "Bill" O'Brien practices exclusively in labor and employment law, with substantial experience in workplace disputes, wrongful termination, employment agreements, noncompete agreements and stock option agreements. Mr. O'Brien's representation often involves legal claims for wrongful termination; whistleblower violations; age, disability, sexual and racial discrimination; and sexual harassment.

Michael B. Bloom is widely recognized for his representation of employees in workers' compensation claims and employment disputes. His representation of employees typically involves work-related injuries and all types of employment claims with an emphasis on disability discrimination, wrongful termination and severance agreements.

MUIR, HEUEL, CARLSON & SPELHAUG, P.A.
404 Marquette Bank Building - P.O. Box 1057 - Rochester, MN 55903
Phone: (507) 288-4110, Fax: (507) 288-4122

Dan Heuel, Ross Muir, James Carlson, Robert Spelhaug

Muir, Heuel, Carlson & Spelhaug, P.A., is unique in southern Minnesota as a firm dedicated exclusively to the representation of individuals and businesses involved in litigation. Founded in 1966 by Ross Muir, the firm has resisted the urge to diversify into a general practice, preferring to remain focused on its trial practice speciality, attracting a reputation as a vigorous and respected advocate for plaintiffs' and defendants' rights. The four partners, supported by a staff of certified legal investigators, handles a wide array of matters ranging from personal injury to construction to employment to professional liability, including medical malpractice.

Ross Muir, with more than 35 years of experience, concentrates on representing injured accident victims and their families and is well recognized for his expertise in accident reconstruction in all phases of civil litigation. He is a member of the Minnesota Trial Lawyers Association and the Minnesota Defense Lawyers Association.

Daniel Heuel joined the firm in 1978 and likewise devotes himself to civil litigation for both plaintiffs and defendants. He has distinguished himself in employment and discrimination law and is Certified as a Civil Trial Specialist by the Minnesota State Bar Association's Civil Litigation Section. He was president of the Minnesota State Bar Association's Third District in 1994-95.

James Carlson joined the firm in 1976 and is especially active in the representation of insurance companies and their insureds, with a strong emphasis on workers' compensation and products liability. He is Certified as a Civil Trial Specialist by the Minnesota State Bar Association's Civil Litigation Section of the Minnesota State Bar Association, a member of the Minnesota Defense Lawyers Association and licensed to practice in Minnesota and Illinois. He has been president of the Rochester Public Utility Board since 1989.

Robert Spelhaug, with the firm since 1980, rounds out the complement of trial specialists with his own certifications with the Minnesota State Bar Association's Civil Litigation Section and the National Board of Trial Advocacy. He is respected for his expertise in medical malpractice and products liability. He served with the United States Army from 1972 to 1974.

Muir, Heuel, Carlson & Spelhaug, P.A., is at the forefront of changes in the law with a strong appellate practice augmented by the latest in computer technology. It is dedicated to retaining its niche as lawyers specialized in trial practice and is well-positioned to bring to bear its experience and knowledge on behalf of clients who are confronted with a need for a trial lawyer.

NICHOLS KASTER & ANDERSON

4644 IDS Center - 80 South Eighth Street - Minneapolis, MN 55402-2242
Phone: (612) 338-1919, Fax: (612) 338-4878,
E-mail: nichols@nka.com, Web Site: www.nka.com

In 1974, Donald Nichols founded a law firm in the IDS dedicated to serving its clients' needs. Through the years, the firm has developed a tradition and well-earned reputation for professionalism and excellence in client service. Today, Nichols Kaster and Anderson continues to build upon this tradition and reputation by delivering timely, responsive and quality legal advice and services to its clients.

The attorneys of Nichols Kaster and Anderson have extensive trial and appellate law experience in both state and federal courts. The firm has successfully handled a wide variety of cases, from its mainstay of sexual harassment and employment discrimination matters to complex class action litigation, wrongful death and high-profile criminal defense cases. The firm's attorneys have achieved statewide and national prominence and recognition, appearing on <I>Nightline, CBS Morning News, Good Morning America<I> and <I>National Public Radio.<I> They have been named "Super Lawyers" by <I>Minnesota Law & Politics<I> and have lectured at the Minnesota Employment Law Institute and more than 100 other seminars for judges and lawyers throughout the United States.

The firm's dedicated staff of professionals and attorneys has as its primary focus the aggressive and effective representation of its clients.

Donald H. Nichols (JD 1971, University of Minnesota) devotes his practice exclusively to trial work. For more than 25 years, his work has attracted national attention. He was one of the first lawyers to challenge the use of polygraphs in the employment setting. Some of his early work defined the right of an employee to change employment despite having confidential information. He brought the first case under the Minnesota Family Act and established one of the longest front pay awards in Minnesota history in the employment setting.

James H. Kaster (JD 1979, Marquette University) has litigated many high-profile cases, including the first verdicts and published decisions in Minnesota on employee polygraphs; the first verdict in Minnesota for minority shareholders in a derivative action; and the first verdict in the nation for liability for exclusive reliance on prayer healing. Mr. Kaster also established the right of Minnesota employees to sue their supervisors for interference with the employment relationship.

J. Poage Anderson (JD 1985 magna cum laude, William Mitchell) is a trial lawyer practicing in general civil and business litigation, farm litigation and personal injury law. He is an accomplished environmental lawyer who has represented individuals, municipalities and corporations in waste water, hazardous waste and highway noise litigation. He has also written extensively on agricultural productivity, soil and water resources and alternative energy development.

REINHARDT & ANDERSON
1000 E. First National Bank Building - 332 Minnesota Street
St. Paul, MN 55101
Phone: (612) 227-9990, Fax: (612) 297-6543

The law firm of Reinhardt & Anderson, founded in 1979 by senior partners Mark Reinhardt and Jeffrey R. Anderson, exclusively represents plaintiffs and primarily specializes in three areas of litigation: personal injury (primarily victims of sexual abuse), employment discrimination and complex commercial litigation. The firm has tried literally hundreds of jury and bench trials, and prides itself on the quality of its attorneys' work, often in cases of first impression. Reinhardt & Anderson attorneys have worked to create or change law with the goal of vindicating and expanding its clients' rights. The firm's philosophy encompasses the values of hard work, ingenuity, integrity, pride in a quality product and carefully calculating risk versus benefit options.

Personal Injury: Reinhardt & Anderson practices extensively in personal injury law, primarily representing sexual abuse victims. Led by Jeffrey R. Anderson, nationally recognized as a leader in pursuing the rights of sexual abuse victims, the firm's attorneys have worked aggressively to liberalize the statute of limitations for sexual abuse victims and have assisted various victims' organizations in passing statutes nationwide that specifically recognize the unique circumstances of sexual abuse cases. The firm represents hundreds of victims nationwide and continues to work to vindicate and empower its clients. The firm often secures substantial settlements for its clients and it has also taken numerous cases to trial, often obtaining six- and seven-figure verdicts.

Employment Discrimination: Five of the firm's thirteen attorneys devote much of their practice to employment discrimination and harassment litigation. The firm has represented multiple plaintiffs in actions against the Minnesota Police Recruitment System, the City of St. Paul and St. Paul Fire Department, and Stroh Brewery Co., as well as the Archdiocese of St. Paul and Minneapolis. The firm represents scores of plaintiffs in other employment actions in both state and federal courts.

Commercial Litigation: Reinhardt & Anderson commercial litigation practice, led by Mark Reinhardt, concentrates its practice primarily in sophisticated litigation, including complex commercial and consumer class actions. Reinhardt & Anderson has represented plaintiff classes in cases involving violations of state and federal antitrust laws, federal racketeering violations, consumer protection laws and securities fraud. Representative commercial cases include: *In Re: Potash Antitrust Litigation; Svenningson v. Piper, Jaffray and Hopwood, et al.* (RICO and Securities fraud class action); *H. J. Inc. v. Northwestern Bell Telephone Co.*, 109 S.Ct. 2893 (1989) (RICO bribery class action); and *In Re: Domestic Air Transportation Litigation* (antitrust price fixing class action).

FELONY & MISDEMEANOR CRIMINAL DEFENSE LAW

This chapter outlines how the criminal justice system operates and describes some of the most common criminal infractions, rights of persons accused of crimes, and crime victims' rights.

CRIMINAL CODES

Criminal law defines conduct that is prohibited and the range of penalties that can be imposed for violating these prohibitions. Persons who violate criminal laws can lose their freedom by either being jailed or imprisoned or, in some states, by being executed. All crimes are defined by statutes. These statutes are collected and organized into codes known as criminal codes. In addition to the Minnesota state criminal code, which applies only in Minnesota, the federal government has a criminal code that regulates certain crimes nationwide. Most criminal activity violates either a state law or a federal law, not both. An important area regulated by both federal and state criminal codes is drug crimes. A person who violates the laws governing controlled substances (which can be illegal drugs such as marijuana and cocaine or a legally prescribed drug such as codeine) can be prosecuted in either state or federal court or both.

Every crime is statutorily defined by a list of elements. In a criminal trial, a prosecutor attempts to prove that all the elements of the crime of which the defendant is accused are met. If a court or jury finds that all the elements of the crime are met, the accused is guilty of the crime.

WHY PUNISH CRIMINALS?

There are a variety of reasons persons committing criminal acts are punished. One reason is retribution. A society outraged by a person's harmful acts often feels the need for revenge, and punishing the criminal tends to satisfy that need. Another reason is deterrence. Sending someone to jail or requiring them to pay a fine may deter not only that person from committing a future crime, but other persons as well. Deterrence is an argument often used in support of the death penalty. A third reason for punishment is incapacitation. For the period of time a criminal is in jail, he or she is off public streets and unable to commit further crimes. Public education is a fourth reason for punishment. The publicity surrounding the trial, conviction and punishment of a criminal educates the public about what is appropriate behavior and the consequences of violating the law. Finally, there is rehabilitation. Criminals who are imprisoned have an opportunity to reevaluate their actions and reshape their values such that when they return to society they are able to function within the boundaries of the law.

OFFENSES

Criminal codes penalize a broad variety of activities. Criminal codes make a major distinction between felonies and misdemeanors. Felonies are crimes for which a person can be sentenced to more than one year in prison. Misdemeanors are divided into three categories: gross misdemeanors, misdemeanors and petty misdemeanors.

ALCOHOL - AND DRUG-RELATED TRAFFIC OFFENSES

Alcohol - and drug-related traffic offenses, commonly known as driving while intoxicated (DWI) offenses, are frequently prosecuted. There are several types of offenses with which a person can be prosecuted as DWI. If a person's blood alcohol content (BAC) is .10 or greater and the person is in physical control of a motor vehicle, he or she is considered to be driving while intoxicated. Even if the BAC is .10 or more within two hours after the person was driving, the same criminal charge applies.

Another type of charge is simply being under the influence of alcohol or drugs. If a person's ability to drive is adversely affected by alcohol or a controlled substance, even if the

BAC is not over the limit, the person is said to be driving under the influence. Generally, if the evidence shows that a person's BAC was .04 or more, that is sufficient to prove he or she was under the influence. It is also a DWI-related crime in Minnesota to refuse to submit to a chemical blood, breath or urine test if the person is asked to do so by a police officer.

DWI laws do not require a person actually to be driving a car to be guilty of the offense. All that is required is that the person be "in physical control" of the vehicle. Physical control can mean sitting in a car, even without the keys in the ignition. Also, the vehicle does not have to be a car. DWI-related offenses can apply to farm tractors or boats.

The first time a person violates any of these provisions is a misdemeanor. However, it is a gross misdemeanor to violate any of the DWI-related provisions twice in five years or three times in ten years. It is also a gross misdemeanor to commit a DWI-related crime while there is a child in the vehicle.

Generally, when a person is convicted of DWI, his or her driver's license will be revoked for 30 days, and a chemical dependency assessment charge of $125 will be imposed. Refusal to submit to alcohol or drug testing will result in automatic license suspension for 90 days. If the person convicted of DWI is under 21 years of age, the license or permit may be revoked for six months. Subsequent offenses bring more severe penalties. When a person commits DWI-related crimes repeatedly, he is described as a "habitual offender," and the penalties for additional offenses increase to include mandatory imprisonment. In some cases, a person who has committed repeated DWI-related crimes may have the following penalties imposed:

- The motor vehicle may be impounded
- The person may be required to abstain from consuming alcohol and controlled substances
- The person may be required to submit to treatment or rehabilitation
- Probation
- The person may lose driving privileges for life

ASSAULT

Minnesota law distinguishes between assault and battery in private lawsuits. Minnesota's criminal code does not distinguish between assault and battery; instead, criminal assault includes both. Assault is defined as an act done with intent to cause another to fear immediate bodily harm or death or intentionally inflicting or attempting to inflict bodily harm on another. Assault is further broken down into degrees depending on whether injury is actually inflicted, the identity of the victim and the degree of injury. The different treatment of assault and battery between the civil and criminal systems can be confusing. For example, attacking someone with a knife is called assault in the criminal code and battery under the civil system. Threatening to attack someone with a knife without actually doing so equals assault under both the criminal and civil codes.

CARJACKING

Carjacking is the forcible or violent taking of a motor vehicle from a person or the owner with the intent of either permanently or temporarily depriving the person or owner of the motor vehicle. Carjacking is a first degree felony.

HARASSMENT AND STALKING

Harassment and stalking are closely related crimes. Harassment and stalking can include:

- Repeated, intrusive, and unwanted acts, words or gestures intended to adversely affect the safety, security or privacy of another
- Targeted residential picketing directed at a particular residence that interferes with the safety, security or privacy of its residents
- Pattern of attending public events after being notified that one's presence is harassing to another
- Repeated unwanted phone calls, letters, telegrams or packages

Harassment and stalking can be difficult to prove, so it is important that a victim try to document the activities as much as possible. Letters, photographs, journal entries describing dates, times, places and witnesses can be helpful in prosecuting a harasser or stalker.

Someone being victimized by a family or household member can seek an order of protection from the district court to protect the victim from abuse. Anyone can ask a state district court for a restraining order to protect himself or herself from anyone else, whether or not the abuser is a family or household member.

THEFT

The legal definition of theft encompasses a broad range of activities when one person uses, transfers, conceals or retains possession of another person's property without the other person's consent. This definition is much broader than what most persons believe to be theft and can include writing bad checks, unauthorized use of a credit card, keeping found property without making a reasonable attempt to find its rightful owner, misusing trade secrets, unlawfully tapping into cable television services, wrongfully receiving public assistance, and removing serial numbers from movable property with the intent of concealing the identity of the true owner.

BURGLARY AND ROBBERY

Burglary is unlawfully breaking into, or remaining in, a building with the intent to commit a crime there. It is burglary to enter a house unlawfully with the intent to steal money or property, but it is also burglary to enter with the intent to commit a felony such as arson or murder. A person commits a burglary regardless of whether he or she actually steals anything or commits any other felony while in the house. Simple robbery is unlawfully taking personal property from another person or in the presence of the other person while using or threatening to use force against the person. Aggravated robbery is robbery committed with a dangerous weapon.

HOMICIDE AND SUICIDE

Homicide is the killing of another human being. There are four types of homicide: murder, voluntary manslaughter, involuntary manslaughter and criminal vehicular homicide.

Murder is the unlawful killing of another with premeditated intent to kill and malice (hatred). Murder is divided into subcategories by degree of seriousness. Murder in the first degree is killing someone with premeditation and intent or during the commission of a violent felony. The amount of premeditation required is very slight, even a moment spent thinking about killing a person before actually killing that person may be sufficient to constitute premeditation. Murder in the second degree is killing someone with intent to kill but without premeditation or killing someone while committing a felony offense. Murder in the third degree is causing the death of another person without intent to kill but through a dangerous act or by distributing a controlled substance.

Manslaughter differs from murder because manslaughter does not require proof of hatred. There are two kinds of manslaughter: voluntary and involuntary. Voluntary manslaughter is killing another person while intentionally engaged in a very dangerous action. Involuntary manslaughter is an unintentional killing; this is usually the result of criminal negligence rather than hatred.

Criminal vehicular homicide is causing the death of another person as a result of negligently operating a motor vehicle.

Suicide is taking one's own life. Suicide and attempted suicide are no longer crimes in Minnesota. However, aiding another person to commit suicide or attempt suicide are crimes. Assisted suicide is a controversial issue that has hotly divided public opinion. In Minnesota, most acts that assist another person to commit suicide are clearly illegal. A few actions are specifically exempted from punishment. For example, withdrawing life support in accordance with a living will or established medical practice is not illegal.

KIDNAPPING

Kidnapping is the forcible and secret abducting, confining or imprisoning of a victim against his or her will with intent to (1) collect a ransom, (2) commit or facilitate the commission of a felony, (3) inflict bodily harm or terrorize the victim, or (4) interfere with any governmental or political function. Kidnapping is a first degree felony. Anyone who kidnaps a child under the age of 13 and commits aggravated child abuse, sexual battery or a lewd act in the presence of the child commits a life felony.

SEX CRIMES

Rape, sodomy, incest, fornication, pimping and prostitution are crimes in Minnesota. Some of these laws, like the prohibitions against sodomy and fornication, are technically still on the books, but rarely enforced. In fact, Minnesota laws are somewhat contradictory because they criminalize sodomy and fornication, but they also make it a crime to discriminate in housing and employment against persons who engage in these activities.

Most persons accused of sex crimes are tried for violations of a modern law that lumps many actions together under the title of criminal sexual conduct. Criminal sexual conduct is divided into four degrees depending upon the age of the victim, age of the accused, whether force is used, and the existence of any special relationship between the parties, such as parent-child or physician-patient.

In Minnesota, judges are required to double the punishment imposed on a pattern sex offender, who is someone who repeats or is likely to repeat a sex crime or someone who plans the crime.

CIVIL RIGHTS CRIMES

The Minnesota Human Rights Act forbids discrimination in employment, housing and commerce on the basis of race, sex, marital status, status with regard to public assistance, disability, sexual orientation or age. Violation of these prohibitions can subject the violator to criminal prosecution.

ATTEMPT, CONSPIRACY, AIDING AND ABETTING

Anyone who, with intent to commit a crime, does an act that is a substantial step toward committing the crime may be guilty of attempting to commit a crime. The substantial step cannot be mere preparation for the crime. For example, if someone buys a gun with intent to kill another person, purchasing the gun is mere preparation and thus is not an attempt. If he or she buys a gun and goes to the other person's house, only to be scared away by the presence of police, he or she may be guilty of attempting to commit a crime. Merely thinking about committing a crime is not a crime.

The law of conspiracy and the law of aiding and abetting are two more general doctrines that apply to a wide range of substantive offenses. Conspiracy is an agreement between two or more persons to commit a crime. A conspirator is considered criminally liable for the acts of co-conspirators if the acts were reasonably foreseeable. If two or more people conspire to commit a crime and at least one of them takes action to further the conspiracy, all parties are guilty of the crime of conspiracy.

Also, a person who aids or advises another in committing a crime can be criminally liable for the acts of the other person. Thus, intentionally advising a person how to commit a crime, for instance, is aiding and abetting. The law treats an aider and abettor as equally liable.

FEDERAL DRUG AND GUN LAWS

Federal laws contain harsh penalties for distributing controlled substances, especially if any firearms are even remotely involved. For example, any person who possesses with intent to distribute five grams of crack cocaine is subject to a mandatory five-year sentence without parole. If a gun is available for use or being carried during a drug transaction, a five-year mandatory sentence must be imposed consecutively to a conviction for any drug offense. The gun does not have to be displayed or used but simply available for use. Thus, if a person possesses five grams of crack cocaine with intent to distribute it from their home and a gun is on the premises, the person would receive a mandatory ten-year sentence, without parole, even for a first offense and even if the offender is only 18 years old. In most circumstances, federal judges cannot depart from these mandatory sentences. Penalties for other controlled substance offenses are also harsh and become much harsher as quantities of the contraband increase.

DEFENSES

In some criminal trials, all the elements of a crime are met but the accused is not punished because he or she has a valid defense to excuse the crime. As a general rule, a person may use whatever force, short of deadly force, he or she reasonably believes is necessary to prevent immediate unlawful harm to self or another person. If a person claims self-defense, the state must prove beyond a reasonable doubt that self-defense was not the motive. A person defending property from interference by others is only allowed to use reasonable force. Using deadly force is only permissible when it reasonably appears necessary to avoid immediate death or serious injury to a person or to prevent the commission of a felony in the actor's dwelling.

Intoxication is not a defense to a crime by itself, but, in rare cases, can prevent a person from being guilty because he or she can not form the necessary intent to commit a crime. For example, someone who is intoxicated probably cannot commit a crime that requires he or she act intentionally, but the intoxicated person may be guilty of another crime that does not require intentional actions.

Except for involuntary manslaughter, anyone who participates in a crime because he or she is coerced with threats that create a reasonable apprehension of immediate death, is excused from criminal liability.

PUNISHMENT

Crimes are divided into categories depending on their seriousness. The most serious crimes, including kidnapping, murder and rape, are called felonies and are subject to the strictest punishment, such as lengthy imprisonment. Lesser crimes are called gross misdemeanors. Still lesser crimes are called misdemeanors. Punishment for committing a misdemeanor or gross misdemeanor may include jail time or fines.

A category below misdemeanors is called petty misdemeanors. Despite their name, petty misdemeanors are not actually crimes under Minnesota law. In Minnesota, petty misdemeanors carry fines of no more than $100 ($200 in a few cases) and a person cannot go to jail for committing a petty misdemeanor. Most minor traffic offenses are petty misdemeanors. Anyone who commits the same petty misdemeanor repeatedly, such as being caught speeding three times within a one-year period, can be charged with a misdemeanor.

Minnesota has laws that allow the authorities to seize property connected with the commission of a crime. For example, Minnesota authorities can seize guns and ammunition found in a vehicle used to commit a felony offense, near a person carrying a felony level amount of drugs, or on the property where a felony-level of drugs is found.

CRIME VICTIM'S RIGHTS

Crime victims have several rights in Minnesota's criminal justice system. The crime victim has a right to be notified of:

- Plea bargain agreements
- When and where the accused will be tried and, if found guilty, sentenced
- Transfer of the offender to a less secure correctional facility
- Release of the offender from prison or other institution
- Evidence indicating the presence of sexually transmitted disease, if victimized by a sexual assault

The crime victim has the following rights in connection with the prosecution of a defendant:

- Right to testify to the court about the crime's impact on the victim
- Right to object to any plea bargain
- Right to give written objection to a sentence
- Right to request a speedy trial
- Right to request court-awarded restitution

The Minnesota Crime Victim Reparations Board can help some crime victims with some financial losses. Victims of violent crimes can ask the board for reimbursement of medical costs, counseling costs, lost wages and other costs associated with the crime. Surviving family members of homicide victims can request aid for funeral expenses, loss of support and counseling. There are several requirements that must be met for a victim to get reimbursement. Victims of most crimes must report the crime to the police within five days of the crime and must cooperate fully in the investigation and prosecution. Most claims must be filed within one year of the victim's injury or death.

The victim can sometimes get the person who committed the crime to pay to replace stolen or damaged property. In this case, the state arranges to collect the money from the criminal and sends a check to the victim when all the restitution has been made. If the court does not order restitution, or if a prosecutor does not press charges, the victim still has the option to sue the person in civil court. Other services available to certain crime victims are battered women's shelters and sexual assault assistance.

JUVENILES AND THE LAW

Minnesota has a juvenile court system for minors under age 18 that operates separately from other courts. Minors who run afoul of the law are said to commit delinquent acts rather than crimes. The distinction is one of words only. Delinquent acts committed by a minor are called crimes if committed by an adult. The most significant distinction between the juvenile court system and adult criminal courts is in courtroom procedures. Juvenile courts are generally less formal than other courts. Juveniles do not have a right to a trial by jury in Minnesota.

Minnesota recently made dramatic changes in how some violent juvenile offenders are treated. A juvenile age 14 to 17 accused of committing a felony can be tried as an adult if the juvenile court finds the accused is dangerous and unsuitable for treatment within the juvenile system. These proceedings are conducted in open court. However, no one under the age of 14 in Minnesota can be tried as an adult, no matter how serious the offense. A juvenile court must make juveniles found guilty of traffic offenses pay reasonable restitution for damage caused by their actions.

Minors giving courtroom testimony in an assault case or other crime of violence such as murder can have a supportive person present during their testimony. This new law greatly expands the conditions under which a supportive person can assist a minor giving testimony.

Minnesota also has established a class of serious juvenile offenders, called the extended jurisdiction juvenile (EJJ). The EJJ has the right to a public defender and a jury trial. EJJs are serious offenders who are sentenced with a juvenile court penalty as well as an adult court penalty. The adult-level penalty is not imposed unless the limitations of the sentence are violated.

FELONY & MISDEMEANOR CRIMINAL DEFENSE

Ayers & Riehm
Firstar Center
Suite 2330
101 East Fifth Street
St. Paul, MN 55101

Phone: (612) 222-8400
Fax: (612) 222-1844

DAVID L. AYERS

DAVID L. AYERS: Mr. Ayers practices primarily in criminal defense, in which he has successfully tried a wide range of criminal cases. In his extensive criminal trial practice, he has represented hundreds of individuals charged with all types of crimes, including assault, child abuse, criminal sexual conduct, criminal vehicular operation, drug possession and sale, DWI, homicide, kidnapping, robbery, theft and white collar offenses. In addition, he is experienced in high-profile cases involving professionals. He assisted in the defense of three of the most infamous first degree murder cases ever brought to trial in Minnesota (*State v. Caldwell, State v. Howard* and *State v. Mikulanec*) and was appointed Special Prosecutor by the St. Paul City Attorney's Office to handle a conflict case. Mr. Ayers is one of eight lawyers in Minnesota to be named in all three categories (Wins the Most Cases; Most Prepared; and Most Courteous) of the Minnesota Judges' Choice Awards. He is profiled in *Who's Who in Criminal Law* and was selected as a Super Lawyer by *Minnesota Law & Politics*. Mr. Ayers lectures nationally and locally to student and lawyer groups on criminal law, criminal procedure and trial tactics.
Education: JD 1978, Hamline University; BA 1975, University of Minnesota.
Admitted: 1979 Minnesota; 1980 U.S. Dist. Ct. (MN); 1982 U.S. Ct. App. (8th Cir.); 1988 Wisconsin.
Employment History: Law Clerk/Associate 1977-82, Thomson & Nordby.
Professional Associations: Minnesota Society of Criminal Justice (past President); Minnesota Association of Criminal Defense Lawyers; MTLA; MSBA; RCBA; NACDL.
Community Involvement: St. Paul Golden Gloves (former boxer, instructor); Mendota Heights Athletic Assn. (former baseball, hockey and softball coach; former Softball Commissioner); St. Joseph's School (softball and swimming coach); Sibley Area Traveling Fastpitch (softball coach); volunteer at various school fund-raising events and parent committees at Cretin-Derham Hall and St. Joseph's School.
Firm: Ayers & Riehm was founded in 1983 by longtime friends Dave Ayers and Harry Riehm. The firm handles primarily criminal defense and plaintiffs' personal injury litigation, and provides trial and appellate legal services in Minnesota and Wisconsin. Harold H. Riehm, senior partner and cofounder, practices in bodily injury and death cases, including auto accidents, workers' compensation, medical malpractice, and liquor and products liability. David R. Newcomb, Jr., a ten-year veteran of the firm, handles general litigation including bankruptcy, business, criminal defense and family law, and workplace and other personal injury law. The firm's lawyers take pride in providing clients with quality, personal service. Client confidence and satisfaction are always paramount at Ayers & Riehm, and client and lawyer referrals are a regular source of business.

Extensive Experience In:
• DWI & Misdemeanor Defense
• Felony Defense
• Juvenile Defense

FELONY & MISDEMEANOR CRIMINAL DEFENSE

Thomas E. Bauer and Associates
701 Fourth Avenue South
Suite 600
Minneapolis, MN 55415-1633

Phone: (612) 337-9555
Fax: (612) 333-2701

THOMAS E. BAUER

THOMAS E. BAUER: Mr. Bauer has a criminal law practice representing individuals in state and federal courts. His experience with defense includes numerous homicides, drug possession and sale, alcohol-related traffic offenses (DWIs), criminal sexual conduct, complex white collar crimes, child abuse and assaults. His cases include: *State v. Williams* murder one (battered woman syndrome); *State v. Hanson,* assault one, kidnapping, partial acquittal (court trial on insanity defense, Post Traumatic Stress Disorder, Vietnam vet, hostage taking at the Minneapolis airport); *In re: T.W.,* arson one, dismissal (juvenile defendant who confessed to the arson of the $90 million Norwest Bank/Donaldson's fire, the largest arson case in Minnesota history); *United States v. Michaeloff,* federal white collar crime (Budget Travel multimillion dollar bust-out scheme); *State v. Hennessy,* forgery, DWI (dismissal of felony in which a postal worker allegedly forged and filed his own death certificate with the court to escape multiple DWI convictions); precharge investigation into Black Tie Limousine (federal money laundering allegations, largest outcall prostitution enterprise in the state as reported by the press). His practice includes precharge representation on the state and federal criminal matters with the purpose of stopping the charging process or eliminating charges in advance. Mr. Bauer has been a speaker at the Criminal Justice Institute, the Minnesota Continuing Legal Education Institute, a Minnesota Trial Lawyers Association Seminar, and he was an instructor at the Minnesota Bureau of Criminal Apprehension Police School.
Education: JD 1974, University of Minnesota; BA 1971, University of Minnesota.
Admitted: 1974 Minnesota; 1975 U.S. Dist. Ct. (MN); 1990 U.S. Ct. App. (8th Cir.).
Employment History: 1983-present, Thomas E. Bauer and Associates; Assistant Hennepin County Public Defender 1980-83; Assistant Hennepin County Attorney 1974-80; Adjunct Professor 1974-80, William Mitchell College of Law; U.S. Army 1966-68.
Representative Clients: Mr. Bauer represents government attorneys and private practice attorneys, law enforcement officers, political officials, professional athletes, business leaders, and radio and entertainment figures.
Professional Associations: MSBA; HCBA; Minnesota Society for Criminal Justice; NACDL; Minnesota County Attorneys' Assn. (past Lobbyist); International Assn. of Arson Investigators (past Member; Lecturer).
Community Involvement: Criminal Sexual Conduct Law enactment volunteer work.

Extensive Experience In:
• Drug Cases
• Sexual Assaults
• Driving While Intoxicated Defenses

FELONY & MISDEMEANOR CRIMINAL DEFENSE

Belfry Law Office, Chartered
6 Thirteenth Street
Cloquet, MN 55720

Phone: (218) 878-0672
Fax: (218) 879-2065

K. SCOTT BELFRY

K. SCOTT BELFRY: Mr. Belfry is a criminal trial lawyer and is Certified as a Criminal Trial Specialist by the National Board of Trial Advocacy. He practices in state and federal courts, and has tried to jury verdict more than 100 criminal cases, including murder, sexual and other assault, robbery, drug, burglary, theft, DWI and criminal vehicular operation. Before turning to criminal defense work, Mr. Belfry was a prosecutor, which gives him a unique insight into the cases he handles. In addition, he has been an instructor in the paralegal program at the University of Wisconsin-Superior.

Education: JD 1979, Hamline University; BA 1974 cum laude, Winona State University; United States Marine Corps 1969-71.

Admitted: 1980 Minnesota; 1982 U.S. Dist. Ct. (MN); 1994 U.S. Ct. App. (8th Cir.).

Employment History: President 1991-present, Belfry Law Office, Chartered; Assistant Public Defender 1987-present, State Board of Public Defense: Partner 1987-91, Rudy, Prevost, Gassert, Yetka, Korman & Belfry; Assistant County Attorney 1981-87, State of Minnesota.

Representative Clients: Mr. Belfry represents people accused of crimes of various magnitude, including murder; people accused of crimes in state and federal courts; and people who are unable to afford a privately retained lawyer.

Professional Associations: Academy of Certified Trial Lawyers of Minnesota 1996-present; MSBA 1987-present; 11th District Bar Assn 1987-present; Carlton County Bar Assn. 1981-present (various positions); NBTA (Criminal Trial Specialist 1988-present).

Community Involvement: ISD 701 School Board 1988-91 (Board of Directors); Cloquet Area Chamber of Commerce 1989-91 (Board of Directors); Assn. of Retarded Citizens— Duluth 1985-87 (Board of Directors; Vice President 1986-87); National Guard Citizens' Committee of Cloquet 1994-present.

Firm: Belfry Law Office, Chartered, is a general practice firm known as the "blue collar guys with ties." The firm represents and advises individuals, organizations and businesses on various legal matters, including real estate purchase and sale, wills, incorporations, employment issues, and civil and criminal litigation. The firm has developed a reputation for a personalized approach to serious legal matters. The firm's lawyers are dedicated to result-oriented solutions that resolve disputes and protect their clients' rights. The firm believes it can deliver quality legal services for reasonable prices. Its criminal representation services are particularly extensive and respected in the legal community.

Extensive Experience In:
• Criminal Pretrial Issues
• Trial Issues/Litigation
• Post-Conviction Issues

FELONY & MISDEMEANOR CRIMINAL DEFENSE

**BAILEY W.
BLETHEN**

Blethen, Gage & Krause, PLLP
127 South Second Street
P.O. Box 3049
Mankato, MN 56002-3049

Phone: (507) 345-1166
Fax: (507) 345-8003

BAILEY W. BLETHEN: Mr. Blethen has a broad litigation practice and has handled numerous civil and criminal trials and appeals. In recent years, his emphasis has been in employment law, commercial litigation and criminal defense. Mr. Blethen is a regular lecturer at Mankato State University on the liability of coaches and trainers.

Education: JD 1963 cum laude, University of Minnesota (Case Editor, *Minnesota Law Review*); AB 1960 cum laude, Brown University.

Admitted: 1963 Minnesota; 1963 U.S. Dist. Ct. (MN); 1970 U.S. Ct. App. (8th Cir.); 1989 U.S. Tax Ct.; 1993 U.S. Sup. Ct.

Employment History: Attorney 1963-present, Blethen, Gage & Krause, PLLP.

Representative Clients: Hickory Tech Corp.; Norwest Bank of Minnesota South Central, N.A.; Graybar Electric; Winco, Inc.; Minnesota Valley Action Council; KFC of Shakopee, Inc.; Waseca Mutual Insurance Company.

Professional Associations: MSBA; MTLA; ATLA; Minnesota Assn. of Criminal Defense Lawyers.

Community Involvement: Mankato State University [Classic Committee (Chair); Maverick Booster Club (Director)]; First Bank Tip-Off Classic Tournament (Chair); YMCA Brother-Sister Program (Advisory Committee); Mankato West High School Sophomore Boys Coach; National Assn. of Basketball Coaches.

Firm: Founded in 1896, Blethen, Gage & Krause, PLLP, is a general practice law firm. *See complete firm profile in the Firm Profiles section.*

FELONY & MISDEMEANOR CRIMINAL DEFENSE

Manahan & Bluth Law Office, Chartered
416 South Front Street
P.O. Box 287
Mankato, MN 56002-0287

Phone: (507) 387-5661
Fax: (507) 387-2111
E-mail: mb_law@ic.mankato.mn.us

JOSEPH P. BLUTH

JOSEPH P. BLUTH: Mr. Bluth concentrates primarily in serious felony cases, including sexual misconduct, environmental, white collar, alcohol (DWI) and drug-related, child abuse and other complex cases. A member of the American Academy of Matrimonial Lawyers, Mr. Bluth handles family law matters with an emphasis on custody disputes and cases involving dysfunction in the family due to alcoholism, addiction, mental or emotional health problems or abuse. His practice also extends to civil litigation, including civil rights, torts, property damage and personal injury. He is very experienced in handling high-profile cases involving professionals, including employment, misconduct, malfeasance and licensing issues. Mr. Bluth is listed in *Who's Who in American Law,* 1996, and *The Best Lawyers in America,* 1997-98.
Education: JD 1977 cum laude, Hamline University; BA 1975, Mankato State University.
Admitted: 1978 Minnesota; 1978 U.S. Dist. Ct. (MN); 1991 Wisconsin; 1994 U.S. Sup. Ct.
Employment History: Partner 1986-present, Manahan & Bluth Law Office, Chartered; Assistant County Attorney 1977-78, Todd County Attorney's Office; United States Army 1968-71—served in Vietnam 1969-71, Citations: Paratrooper, Bronze Star, Army Medal of Commendation.
Professional Associations: American Academy of Matrimonial Lawyers [Minnesota Chapter (President-elect; Board of Governors; Treasurer 1994; Secretary 1995)]; Minnesota Society for Criminal Justice (past President); ATLA [(Family Law Section (Chair 1995)]; MTLA; NACDL; Todd County Child Protection Team (past Member).
Community Involvement: Litchfield Chapter of Rotary International (past President); Cub Scouts (past Packmaster for Troop 98); School District 77 (Lecturer, Art Masterpiece).
Firm: Founded in 1972, Manahan & Bluth Law Office, Chartered, is a professional corporation specializing in complex civil and criminal trial work, including automobile accidents, environmental, white collar crime and family law. The firm has handled numerous appeals to the Supreme Court and serves clients in southern Minnesota and Wisconsin. Manahan & Bluth Law Office, Chartered, uses advanced computers and a vast network of resources to assist in difficult cases. The firm's staff is adept at communications and the use of technology to provide cost-effective service. *See complete firm profile in the Firm Profiles section.*

FELONY & MISDEMEANOR CRIMINAL DEFENSE

Frederic Bruno & Associates
5500 Wayzata Boulevard
Suite 730
Minneapolis, MN 55416

Phone: (612) 545-7900
Fax: (612) 545-0834
E-mail: bruno@brunolaw.com

FREDERIC BRUNO

FREDERIC BRUNO: Mr. Bruno practices exclusively in criminal defense, including trial and appeals, with emphasis on complex and problematic cases. He is the author of numerous articles, including "Victims' Rights: Trial by Tribulation," *Bench & Bar,* November 1995; and "Disorder in the Court: Probation Violations in Minnesota," *Challenger,* Summer 1993.

Education: JD 1980, St. Louis University; BA 1977, Stanford University.

Admitted: 1980 Minnesota; 1980 U.S. Dist. Ct. (MN).

Employment History: Owner 1980-present, Frederic Bruno & Associates; Law Clerk 1978-80, Law Office of Thomas R. Green, St. Louis, MO; Law Clerk 1978, Rhode Island Attorney General (major felony prosecution).

Representative Clients: Mr. Bruno has had successful outcomes to the following high-profile cases: *U.S. v. Bolstad, Nichols and Newhouse* (savings and loan fraud); *U.S. v. Anderson* (money laundering); *State v. Susan Green* (election fraud, perjury); *State v. Clausen* (controlled substance penalties); *State v. Lov* (bond reinstatement); *State v. Pham* (evidence recovery, murder); *State v. Moran* (boating while intoxicated); *South Dakota In re J.A.* (manslaughter); *State v. Gilbert* (felony assault on police officer); *State v. Grengs* (gang rape); *State v. Officer David Peterson* (felony assault on suspect).

Professional Associations: MSBA [Criminal Section (Chair 1993-94); *Criminal Law News* (Editor-in-Chief)]; HCBA (Criminal Committee); Minnesota Society for Criminal Justice (past President); NACDL; Minnesota Assn. of Criminal Defense Lawyers; MTLA; Criminal Justice Institute (Faculty 1993); Minnesota Traffic Law Institute (Faculty 1993-94).

Community Involvement: University of Minnesota Law School [Judicial Trial Skills Training Program (Faculty)]; Hamline University Law School [ABA Criminal Trial Competition (Advisor)]; Referee 1985-present, Hennepin County District Court.

Firm: Frederic Bruno & Associates and its predecessor firms have been actively engaged in criminal defense for more than 17 years. Mr. Bruno is an instructor for the Minnesota Continuing Legal Education program; is a frequent speaker at criminal law seminars for attorneys, prosecutors and judges; and has been a commentator on WCCO radio as well as Minnesota Public Radio. All personnel in the firm are dedicated to criminal defense, including Timothy R. Anderson, an Associate Attorney and a 1993 cum laude graduate of the University of Minnesota Law School. *See complete firm profile in the Firm Profiles section.*

Extensive Experience In:
• Assault Trials
• Drug Cases
• Search & Seizure

FELONY & MISDEMEANOR CRIMINAL DEFENSE

Cahill Law Office
150 South Broadway Avenue
Wayzata, MN 55391-1701
Phone: (612) 449-9822
Fax: (612) 449-0167
800: (888) 449-9822
E-mail: CahillLaw@aol.com

PETER A. CAHILL

PETER A. CAHILL: Mr. Cahill currently practices almost exclusively in criminal defense law. He began his career as a full-time Hennepin County Assistant Public Defender in 1984, handling all aspects of adult felony and misdemeanor defense. Since his move to private practice in 1987, he has concentrated his practice in defense of homicide cases, sex crimes and DWI. He also handles white collar crime, drug, traffic and misdemeanor cases. In addition to his defense experience, Mr. Cahill is a former prosecutor for the City of St. Louis Park. Mr. Cahill is also a former adjunct professor in legal writing for William Mitchell College of Law and a former clinical instructor (domestic abuse prosecution clinic) at the University of Minnesota Law School. He is a frequent lecturer on criminal topics for Minnesota Continuing Legal Education and has been a guest lecturer at trial advocacy courses at the University of Minnesota Law School.
Education: JD 1984, University of Minnesota (Order of the Coif); BA 1981, University of Minnesota.
Admitted: 1984 Minnesota; 1987 U.S. Dist. Ct. (MN); 1988 U.S. Dist. Ct. (E. Dist. WI); 1992 U.S. Dist. Ct. (W. Dist. WI); 1993 U.S. Ct. App. (8th Cir.); 1989 U.S. Sup. Ct.; Pro hac vice appearances in Wisconsin, Texas and South Dakota courts.
Employment History: Owner 1993-present, Cahill Law Office; Partner 1988-93, Colich & Cahill; Associate 1987-88, Colich & Wieland; Assistant Public Defender 1984-87, Hennepin County.
Representative Clients: Mr. Cahill represents individuals charged with felonies and DWI, but handles a wide variety of criminal defense cases. While he does practice in federal court, the bulk of his practice is in state court.
Professional Associations: MSBA [Criminal Law Section (past Board of Governors)]; HCBA [Criminal Law Section (past Governing Council)]; NACDL (past Member); Minnesota Assn. of Criminal Defense Lawyers (past Member); MTLA (past Member).
Community Involvement: Cub Scout Leader 1991-present; St. Philip the Deacon Church (Sharing and Caring Hands Volunteer Coordinator 1994-96); St. Bartholomew's Catholic Church 1996-present [Partnership Committee (Chair); Religious Education Teacher]; Minnesota Judicial Trial Skills Training Program (Volunteer; Community Speaker).
Firm: The Cahill Law Office was founded as a sole practice in 1993. The firm practices almost entirely in criminal defense law, but also handles a small amount of civil litigation for its criminal defense clients. The firm also has a close working relationship with Theresa White, an experienced criminal defense lawyer who concentrates her practice defending women charged with crimes.

Extensive Experience In:
• Murder Defense
• Sex Crimes Defense
• DWI

FELONY & MISDEMEANOR CRIMINAL DEFENSE

Allan Hart Caplan & Associates
525 Lumber Exchange Building
10 South Fifth Street
Minneapolis, MN 55402

Phone: (612) 341-4570
Fax: (612) 341-0507

ALLAN HART
CAPLAN

ALLAN HART CAPLAN: Mr. Caplan began his career in 1974 as an Assistant Hennepin County Attorney. He developed extensive experience prosecuting all types of felony cases for six years, two of which were spent prosecuting major white collar crime. In 1976, Mr. Caplan directed the prosecution of a Boston Bruins hockey player who was charged with a felony assault resulting from an altercation with a Minnesota North Stars player during a hockey game. Due to that case, Mr. Caplan authored "Sports Violence and the Criminal Prosecution," for *Trial* magazine. In 1980, Mr. Caplan began his career as a defense lawyer. He has successfully represented hundreds of clients in all types of criminal cases, from DWI and domestic assault to drug cases, sex crimes and murder one.
Education: JD 1974, William Mitchell; BA 1966, University of Minnesota.
Admitted: 1974 Minnesota; 1975 U.S. Dist. Ct. (MN); 1988 Wisconsin; 1992 U.S. Dist. Ct. (AZ).
Employment History: Founder 1983-present, Allan Hart Caplan & Associates; Assistant Public Defender 1980-83, Hennepin County Public Defender's Office; Assistant Hennepin County Attorney 1974-80, Hennepin County Attorney's Office.
Representative Clients: Mr. Caplan has represented numerous clients in all areas of criminal defense, including murder, drugs, sex crimes, assaults, thefts, white collar crime and DWIs.
Professional Associations: ABA 1984-present; HCBA 1984-present; MSBA 1984-present; NACDL 1985-present; National Assn. of District Attorneys 1973.
Community Involvement: Juvenile Diabetes Foundation, Minnesota 1979-present (President 1979-81; Board of Directors 1990-present).
Firm: Founded in 1983, Allan Hart Caplan & Associates has become one of the largest criminal defense firms in the midwestern United States. With five attorneys, one of whom is always on call, the firm is available at a moment's notice to answer inquiries or to deal with custodial situations 24 hours a day, 7 days a week, 365 days a year. Since its inception, the firm has represented more than 3,500 clients in all types of criminal matters, from drunk driving and assaults to drug cases and murder one. The firm has extensive experience in all facets of criminal defense, from precharge or preindictment representation through plea negotiations and trial and appeals in state and federal courts. Two of the firm's members are former prosecutors. Access to and the ability to use the latest technology permits the firm to respond instantly to any conceivable criminal defense problem.

FELONY & MISDEMEANOR CRIMINAL DEFENSE

Cleary Law Office
25 Constitution Avenue
Suite 105
445 Minnesota Street
St. Paul, MN 55155

Phone: (612) 296-3952
Fax: (612) 297-5801

EDWARD J. CLEARY

EDWARD J. CLEARY: Mr. Cleary is a trial and appellate lawyer concentrating on felony defense in state courts, white collar investigations and defense in federal court, and First Amendment litigation and appeals at state and federal levels. He has won at the trial level (homicide acquittal), at the state appellate level (on Fourth Amendment grounds), and before the United States Supreme Court (on First Amendment grounds). He is a nationally known author and lecturer, having won an award from the American Library Association for writing the best book on intellectual freedom in the nation in 1994 and 1995 (*Beyond the Burning Cross: The First Amendment and the Landmark R.A.V. Case*, Random House 1994, Vintage 1995). Mr. Cleary has lectured frequently on constitutional law issues to various organizations including the ABA National Convention, Northwestern School of Law, Washington and Lee Law School, Stanford Law School as well as at local schools and colleges.

Education. JD 1977, University of Minnesota; BA 1974 magna cum laude, University of Minnesota.

Admitted: 1977 Minnesota; 1977 U.S. Dist. Ct. (MN); 1981 U.S. Ct. App. (8th Cir.); 1981 U.S. Sup. Ct.

Employment History: 1980-present, Cleary Law Offices; Attorney 1980-95, Ramsey County Public Defender's Office; Attorney 1978-80, Chief Judge D.D. Wozniak (Retired).

Professional Associations: NACDL; Minnesota Assn. of Criminal Defense Lawyers; Minnesota Advocates for Human Rights; PEN Center USA; RCBA (Ethics Committee 1990-93; Executive Council 1993-96; Vice President 1996-97; President-Elect 1997-98).

Community Involvement: St. Paul Charter Commission 1994-96.

FELONY & MISDEMEANOR CRIMINAL DEFENSE

Colich & Associates
10 South Fifth Street
Suite 420
Minneapolis, MN 55402
Phone: (612) 333-7007
Fax: (612) 333-0492

MICHAEL J.
COLICH

MICHAEL J. COLICH: Mr. Colich is a distinguished criminal defense attorney practicing in both federal and state courts. His clients include corporations, companies, directors and officers as well as individuals charged with complex white collar crimes, serious felonies and misdemeanor offenses, such as money laundering, civil rights violations, murder, criminal vehicular homicide, sexual misconduct, child abuse, assault, drugs, theft and driving while intoxicated. Mr. Colich has represented more than 30 individuals charged with murder. His major cases include: *State v. Brown* (first degree murder); *State v. Caline* (first degree murder); *State v. Quinn* (Minnesota North Stars player); *State v. Greene* (second degree murder); *State v. Welle* (Majority Leader, Minnesota House of Representatives); *U.S. v. Sauro* (Minneapolis police officer); *U.S. v. University of Minnesota* (fraud); and *U.S. v. Alexander* (drugs). In addition, Mr. Colich handles cases under investigation and has been successful in avoiding the issuance of charges. Mr. Colich tried more than 90 major felonies as an Assistant Hennepin County Attorney. He was selected as a "Minnesota Top Trial Attorney" by *Minnesota Judges and Trial Lawyers* and "Most Courteous Attorney, Most Well-Prepared and Wins Most Cases" by the Minnesota Lawyers Judges Choice Awards. In addition, he is a speaker at the Minnesota Continuing Legal Education's Criminal Justice Institute.
Education: JD 1977 with honors, Pepperdine University; BA 1974, University of Minnesota.
Admitted: 1977 Minnesota.
Employment History: 1984-present, Colich & Associates; Assistant Hennepin County Attorney 1977-84, Hennepin County Criminal Division.
Representative Clients: Representation includes attorneys from both the private and public sector, police officers, political figures and business leaders, as well as high-profile sports figures from professional baseball, hockey, football and basketball teams.
Professional Associations: MSBA; HCBA; ABA; Minnesota Court Advisory Committee on Rules of Criminal Procedure.
Firm: Colich & Associates was founded in 1984 along with Lucy A. Wieland, a current Hennepin County District Judge. For more than 13 years, the firm has represented clients in Minnesota and throughout the United States. The firm exclusively handles criminal defense.

FELONY & MISDEMEANOR CRIMINAL DEFENSE

Thornton, Hegg, Reif, Johnston & Dolan, P.A.
1017 Broadway
P.O. Box 819
Alexandria, MN 56308-0819
Phone: (320) 762-2361
Fax: (320) 762-1638
E-mail: thrjd@alexandria.polaristel.net

MICHAEL J. DOLAN

MICHAEL J. DOLAN: Mr. Dolan has been practicing criminal law since 1983. He has served as assistant county attorney, city attorney and special prosecutor. In addition, he served as assistant state public defender and assistant county public defender. Mr. Dolan represents individuals in criminal actions and many of his criminal clients are referrals from other attorneys. Mr. Dolan is Certified as a Civil Trial Specialist by the Minnesota State Bar Association. In addition to his criminal practice, he has a significant practice in family law and civil litigation matters, including the representation of individuals and businesses in employment law matters. Mr. Dolan serves frequently as a mediator or arbitrator chosen by plaintiffs and defendants to resolve disputes, including auto accidents, construction, contract and marital divorce cases. Mr. Dolan serves as an adjudicator attorney for Legal Services of Northwest Minnesota, providing primarily family law services to clients with financial limitations. He was recently recognized by Legal Services of Northwest Minnesota as their Advocacy Achievement Award winner for 1996. As with the other members of his firm, Mr. Dolan believes that effective representation is built upon a reputation of hard work, zealous advocacy and a willingness to try cases.

Education: JD 1983 cum laude, Hamline University; BA 1980 cum laude, Hamline University (Pi Gamma Mu; Department Honors in Philosophy).

Admitted: 1983 Minnesota; 1983 U.S. Dist. Ct. (MN); 1986 U.S. Sup. Ct.

Employment History: Partner 1987-present, Thornton, Hegg, Reif, Johnston & Dolan, P.A., Assistant Public Defender 1986-90, Douglas County, Minnesota; Assistant Douglas County Attorney 1984-86, Douglas County, Minnesota.

Representative Clients: Mr. Dolan represents individuals involved in criminal matters and family law actions, wrongfully injured persons and government officials. He is city attorney for five cities, special prosecutor for Douglas County, and provides individual representation to other government officials. Mr. Dolan also represents individual businesses including service organizations in connection with employment matters. He also serves as mediator or arbitrator as chosen by plaintiffs and defendants. A significant portion of Mr. Dolan's criminal work comes from lawyers who refer their clients and families to him.

Professional Associations: Douglas County Bar Assn. 1983-present (President 1995-96; Treasurer 1994-95; CLE Coordinator 1995-96), Seventh Judicial District Bar Assn. 1983-present; MSBA 1983-present; ATLA 1995-present.

Community Involvement: Northwest Minnesota Legal Services 1986-present; Douglas County Developmental Achievement Center 1994-present (Treasurer; past President). *See complete firm profile in the Firm Profiles section.*

Extensive Experience In:
- Criminal Law
- Family Law/Divorce
- Employment Law

FELONY & MISDEMEANOR CRIMINAL DEFENSE

Eller Law Office
925 First Street South
St. Cloud, MN 56302

Phone: (320) 253-3700
Fax: (320) 253-5105

DANIEL A. ELLER

DANIEL A. ELLER: Mr. Eller has more than 20 years of experience in criminal and civil trial practice in central Minnesota. In addition to his private practice, he served as public defender from 1973 through 1990, with 13 years as district public defender for the Seventh Judicial District. In both his private practice and as a public defender, Mr. Eller has represented individuals charged with murder, assault, robbery, criminal sexual conduct, drug-related crimes and alcohol-related traffic offenses. Mr. Eller has tried cases of statewide notoriety, including *State v. Karr* (pipe bomber) and *State v. Rairdon* (first degree murder). Some of his successful defenses include *State v. Neu* (first degree murder); *State v. Barnes* (attempted first degree murder); *State v. Morris* (attempted first degree murder); *State v. Brist* (first degree murder); and *State v. Wipper* (first degree murder). Since resigning as district public defender in 1990, Mr. Eller has continued his private practice in St. Cloud, specializing in criminal defense. His practice also includes civil trial and family law. He is a frequent guest speaker at local schools and organizations covering legal topics and concerns, a lecturer at St. Cloud State University and an instructor in criminal law at St. John's University.

Education: JD 1969, Georgetown University; BA 1965, St. John's University.

Admitted: 1970 Minnesota; 1970 U.S. Dist. Ct. (MN).

Employment History: Private Practice, 1970-present; Seventh District Public Defender, 1976-90; Law Clerk 1969-70, Honorable Miles Lord, United States District Court, District of Minnesota.

Community Involvement: Mr. Eller has volunteered his time to various charitable and service organizations.

FELONY & MISDEMEANOR CRIMINAL DEFENSE

Attorney at Law
1400 Alworth Building
306 West Superior Street
Duluth, MN 55802

Phone: (218) 722-7813
Fax: (218) 726-1220

DAVID C. KEEGAN

DAVID C. KEEGAN: Mr. Keegan has been providing quality criminal defense representation in northern Minnesota for 19 years. His practice is exclusively criminal defense related litigation primarily in the state trial courts in northern Minnesota, although he occasionally appears in the federal trial court and Minnesota State Appellate Courts. The Keegan Law Office is presently located in Duluth. Mr. Keegan has been Certified as a Criminal Trial Specialist in Criminal Trial Advocacy by the National Board of Trial Advocacy since May 1986. Mr. Keegan has conducted seminars on criminal litigation topics and trial skills for others in the criminal law field. He represents and has represented persons charged with all types of criminal offenses, with concentration on representing persons charged with serious felony offenses.

Education: JD 1978, William Mitchell; BA 1974, University of Minnesota.

Admitted: 1978 Minnesota; 1980 U.S. Dist. Ct. (MN); 1982 U.S. Ct. App. (MN)

Employment History. Private Practice 1981-present; Public Defender Practice 1987-present, Sixth Judicial District Public Defender's Office, Duluth; Public Defender Practice 1981-86, Sixth Judicial District Public Defender's Office, Virginia/Eveleth, MN; Staff Attorney 1978-81, Indian Legal Assistance Program in northeastern Minnesota.

Representative Clients: Mr. Keegan has represented a variety of professional clients in criminal proceedings including doctors, lawyers, accountants, police officers, teachers, union members, clergy, business leaders and occasionally a business organization or corporation in need of criminal law consultation and advice.

Professional Associations: Academy of Certified Trial Lawyers of Minnesota; Minnesota Assn. of Criminal Defense Lawyers; NACDL; MSBA (Criminal Law Section); Eleventh District Bar Assn.; Duluth Trial Lawyers Assn.; NBTA (Criminal Trial Specialist).

Community Involvement: Arrowhead Lawyers Care/Volunteer Attorney Program (Continuing Participant; Volunteer Lawyer of the Year 1988); informal consultation by the NAACP.

Extensive Experience In:
- Criminal Sexual Conduct
- Drug Charges
- Traffic/DWI

FELONY & MISDEMEANOR CRIMINAL DEFENSE

Lund & Patterson
Historic Kelly Building
7 Fourth Street SE
Rochester, MN 55904

Phone: (507) 288-9122
Fax: (507) 288-7753

KEVIN A. LUND

KEVIN A. LUND: Mr. Lund has more than 15 years of experience as a criminal defense trial lawyer in state and federal courts, concentrating in serious felony cases including murder, assault, criminal vehicular homicide, criminal sexual conduct, embezzlement, alcohol and drug-related offenses and other complex cases. He also handles criminal appellate court cases and has argued a number of high-profile appeals with statewide and national significance before the Minnesota Court of Appeals (*State v. Aarsvold,* felony murder/injection of cocaine; *State v. Hawkins,* constitutionality of drug interdiction road block); the Minnesota Supreme Court (*State v. Merrill,* constitutionality of fetal homicide statute); and the Eighth Circuit Court of Appeals (*U.S. v. Moore,* HIV-positive defendant accused of assault). During his years of practice, Mr. Lund has successfully served hundreds of clients in southeastern Minnesota.

Education: JD 1980, Hamline University; BA 1977, University of Minnesota.

Admitted: 1981 Minnesota; 1984 U.S. Dist. Ct. (MN); 1990 U.S. Sup. Ct.

Employment History: Partner 1993-present, Lund & Patterson; 1989-93, Patterson-Restovich-Lund Law Offices, Ltd.; 1981-89, Patterson-Restovich Law Offices, Ltd.

Representative Clients: Mr. Lund represents citizens charged in all types of felony, gross misdemeanor and juvenile crimes.

Professional Associations: Olmsted County Bar Assn.; Minnesota Assn. of Criminal Defense Lawyers.

Community Involvement: Rochester Board of Education; Rochester Historic Preservation Committee (Chair); Olmsted County Historical Society; Rochester Community Youth Basketball (past President); Community Youth Mentorship Program (past President); Community Food Response; Sheriff's Civil Service Commission; Charter Commission; 21st Century Partnership; St. John's Church (Lector).

Firm: Lund & Patterson is a general practice law firm with an emphasis in criminal defense, family law, workers' compensation and business law.

Extensive Experience In:
• Criminal Sexual Conduct
• Search & Seizure
• Alcohol/Drug-Related Offenses

FELONY & MISDEMEANOR CRIMINAL DEFENSE

Attorney at Law
386 North Wabasha Street
Suite 780
St. Paul, MN 55102

Phone: (612) 227-6549
Fax: (612) 224-6151

ROBERT G.
MALONE

ROBERT G. MALONE: Mr. Malone specializes in criminal defense and is one of nineteen Certified Criminal Trial Specialists in the state. He has more than twenty jury acquittals on cases including first degree murder, bank fraud, sexual misconduct, assault of all varieties, theft and DWI. Mr. Malone practices in state and federal courts at the trial and appellate levels.

Education: JD 1978, William Mitchell; BA 1974, University of Minnesota.

Admitted: 1978 Minnesota; 1979 U.S. Dist. Ct (MN); 1989 U.S. Ct. App. (8th Cir.); 1993 U.S. Ct. App. (7th Cir.)

Employment History: 1989-present, Robert G. Malone Law Office (after leaving practice with Joseph S. Friedberg).

Representative Clients: In addition to representing a variety of professional clients in criminal and professional misconduct cases, Mr. Malone has considerable experience representing union members in labor incidents.

Professional Associations: MSBA; RCBA; MTLA; NACDL; Minnesota Assn. of Criminal Defense Lawyers [Lawyers Strike Force (Cochair)]; Minnesota Society for Criminal Justice; Federal Defender Panel.

FELONY & MISDEMEANOR CRIMINAL DEFENSE

**JAMES H.
MANAHAN**

Manahan & Bluth Law Office, Chartered
416 South Front Street
P.O. Box 287
Mankato, MN 56002-0287

Phone: (507) 387-5661
Fax: (507) 387-2111
E-mail: mb_law@ic.mankato.mn.us

JAMES H. MANAHAN: With more than 30 years of experience, Mr. Manahan is nationally Certified as both a Civil Trial Specialist and a Criminal Trial Specialist by the National Board of Trial Advocacy. He was Dean of the Academy of Certified Trial Lawyers of Minnesota, and is a member of the Minnesota Trial Lawyers Association's Board of Governors. He has been listed in *The Best Lawyers in America* since 1993. He has handled 38 appeals to the state and federal appellate courts, and is a Life Fellow of the American Bar Foundation. He defended the only two murder cases in Minnesota that were televised, *State v. Krautkremer* and *State v. Schweim.*

Education: JD 1961, Harvard Law School; AB 1958, Harvard College.

Admitted: 1961 Minnesota; 1972 U.S. Sup. Ct.; 1989 Hawaii; 1990 Colorado.

Professional Associations: MTLA (Board of Governors); American Academy of Matrimonial Lawyers [Minnesota Chapter (National Board; past President)]; Academy of Certified Trial Lawyers of Minnesota (past Dean); American Bar Foundation (Life Fellow).

Community Involvement: Minnesota Civil Liberties Union (Vice President); Common Cause in Minnesota (past Chair); Kiwanis International (Lieutenant. Governor 1992-93); American Arbitration Assn. (Arbitrator); Harvard Law School Assn. of Minnesota (past President); Appointed by Minnesota Supreme Court to State Board of Legal Certification.

Firm: Founded in 1972, Manahan & Bluth Law Office, Chartered, is a professional corporation specializing in complex civil and criminal trial work, including automobile accidents, environmental and white collar crime, and family law. The firm has handled numerous appeals to the Supreme Court, and serves clients in southern Minnesota and Wisconsin. Manahan & Bluth Law Office, Chartered, uses advanced computers and a vast network of resources to assist in difficult cases. The firm's staff is adept at communications and the use of technology to provide cost-effective service. *See complete firm profile in the Firm Profiles section.*

F E L O N Y   &   M I S D E M E A N O R   C R I M I N A L   D E F E N S E

Mauzy Law Firm
Norwest Center
Suite 2885
90 South Seventh Street
Minneapolis, MN 55402
Phone: (612) 340-9108
Fax: (612) 340-1628

WILLIAM J. MAUZY

WILLIAM J. MAUZY: Mr. Mauzy specializes in criminal defense related litigation. He is included in all editions of *The Best Lawyers in America* and his 24-year record of success includes representing individuals and businesses in more than 100 trials in state and federal courts. Mr. Mauzy represents clients in all stages of complex criminal matters in state and federal courts, including cases involving the Foreign Corrupt Practice Act, RICO, antitrust, securities, health care, customs, tax, government procurement and bank fraud. He has successfully tried many less complex but difficult cases including *State v. Lucy Tisland* (first successful battered woman self-defense murder trial in Minnesota); *United States v. Zollie Green* (Minneapolis city councilman acquitted of bribery and other charges); *State v. Quick* and *State v. Roverud* (CEOs of construction companies acquitted of bid-rigging), as well as helped many clients avoid indictment. His recent post-indictment trial successes include *United States v. Zeller et al.* (defendant and his corporation acquitted of all 97 felony counts of mail and ERISA fraud, false statements and conspiracy); *United States v. ION Electronics, et al.* (client acquitted of defense contract procurement fraud); *United States v. Hoffman, et al.* (defense contractor CEO acquitted of unlawful distribution of explosive materials, false statements and conspiracy); *State v. Blomberg* (defendant acquitted of gambling and tax fraud); *United States v. Durenberger, et al.* (prosecution of Senator Durenberger, client, codefendant, dismissed with prejudice); *State v. Sackmaster* (defendant acquitted of sexual misconduct in the workplace); *United States v. Hemmingson, et al.* (in Office of Independent Counsel investigation of former Secretary of Agriculture Mike Espy, former CEO of crop insurance company acquitted of conspiracy to defraud and false statement to federal agencies, false books and records, and securities fraud in Washington, D.C.). Mr. Mauzy is the author of numerous published articles and seminars on criminal law.
Education: JD 1973 cum laude, University of Minnesota; BA 1969, Carleton College.
Admitted: 1973 Minnesota; 1975 U.S. Ct. App. (8th Cir.); 1976 U.S. Sup. Ct.; 1986 U.S. Tax Ct.
Professional Associations: Minnesota Supreme Court Advisory Committee on Rules of Criminal Procedure 1981-present; U.S. District Court, District of Minnesota (Federal Practice Committee 1985-present); HCBA 1975-present (Criminal Law Committee); MSBA (past President 1979-80; Criminal Law Section); ABA (Litigation Section; Criminal Justice Section; Complex Crimes Committee 1983-present); Federal Bar Assn.; MTLA; Academy of Certified Trial Lawyers of Minnesota; Minnesota Assn. of Criminal Defense Lawyers (Board of Directors 1991-94); NACDL (President's Commendation 1979).

FELONY & MISDEMEANOR CRIMINAL DEFENSE

GORDON G. (JEFF)
MOHR

Gordon G. (Jeff) Mohr Law Offices
5001 West 80th Street
Suite 1020
Southgate Office Building
Bloomington, MN 55417

Phone: (612) 831-8700
Fax: (612) 831-6625

GORDON G. (JEFF) MOHR: Mr. Mohr practices primarily in criminal defense. His experience with offenses includes homicide, possession and sale of drugs, alcohol-related traffic offenses, criminal sexual conduct, theft-related offenses, fraud, forgery, all traffic matters, environmental crimes, and other white collar crimes. He has also prosecuted police misconduct litigation for individuals who have suffered harm because of improper action of public officials, including police officers and matters involving excessive force or when police officers have deprived someone of other constitutionally protected rights. Mr. Mohr is a frequent lecturer on DWI trial cases for Minnesota Continuing Legal Education and a former adjunct professor in the criminal clinical programs at William Mitchell and Hamline University law schools. In addition, he is a former instructor of "Use of Deadly Force and Trial Tactics" at the Law Enforcement Training Center; "Prosecution and Defense of Crime" at Northwestern University School of Law; and "Vehicular Homicide and Driving Under the Influence of Alcohol or Drugs" at Northwestern University Traffic Institute. Mr. Mohr is a frequent guest lecturer on the Bloomington Police cable television show, *Laws in Perspective*. In 1980, he received the Certificate of Achievement from the Minnesota Institute of Criminal Justice.

Education: JD 1977, William Mitchell; BA 1973, University of Minnesota.
Admitted: 1977 Minnesota; 1981 U.S. Dist. Ct. (MN).
Employment History: 1984-present, Gordon G. (Jeff) Mohr Law Offices; Chief Prosecutor 1977-84, City of Bloomington.
Representative Clients: Mr. Mohr represents individuals including several professional or former professional athletes; businesses, including establishments holding licenses threatened by governmental action; and several local corporations, their officers and employees.
Professional Associations: ABA 1977-present; MSBA (Criminal Law Committee 1978-present); HCBA [Criminal Law Committee (past Vice Chair)]; Minnesota Society for Criminal Justice; Police Misconduct Litigation Assn.
Community Involvement: Bloomington Crime Prevention Assn. (past President; Board of Directors).
Firm: Gordon G. (Jeff) Mohr Law Offices has an Of Counsel relationship with Henry Wieland (practicing in areas of criminal defense and police misconduct) and Michael J. Hollenhorst (practicing in areas of criminal defense, personal injury and business law).

FELONY & MISDEMEANOR CRIMINAL DEFENSE

Daniel M. Mohs & Associates, Ltd.
The Colonnade
Suite 1025
5500 Wayzata Boulevard
Minneapolis, MN 55416

Phone: (612) 591-1616
Fax: (612) 591-1653

DANIEL M. MOHS

DANIEL M. MOHS: Mr. Mohs is a criminal defense attorney who represents clients charged with serious felonies, including murder and assault charges, drug charges, sex offenses, theft offenses and white collar crimes.

Education: JD 1982, Seattle University; BA 1976, Hamline University

Admitted: 1984 Minnesota; U.S. Dist. Ct. (MN).

Employment History: Mr. Mohs has practiced exclusively in criminal defense since 1987. He has worked as a law clerk for United States Magistrate Judges J. Earl Cudd and Floyd E. Boline and for the law firms of Burns & Zahorsky and Mayo & Norris.

Representative Clients: Mr. Mohs represented Richard Lory at trial in Bemidji on murder charges stemming from his daughter Heather's rape. He also represented Paul Wilson at trial in one of the first cases charged under Minnesota's "pattern of domestic abuse" statute mandating a life sentence for first degree murder. Mr. Mohs has appeared on *Phil Donahue* and *Maury Povich* to discuss specific criminal cases he has handled.

Professional Associations: Minnesota Assn. of Criminal Defense Lawyers; NACDL; MTLA; HCBA; MSBA; ABA; The Order of Barristers; American Judicature Society.

Firm: Founded in 1989, Daniel M. Mohs & Associates, Ltd., is a law firm dedicated to defending the civil and constitutional rights of those arrested or accused of a crime. The firm has represented clients at the trial and appellate court levels in state, federal and juvenile courts in a number of jurisdictions, including Minnesota, Wisconsin, Iowa, North Dakota, South Dakota, Washington, California and Arizona.

FELONY & MISDEMEANOR CRIMINAL DEFENSE

JEFFREY B. RING

Jeffrey B. Ring & Associates
The Interchange Tower
Suite 1690
600 South Highway 169
Minneapolis, MN 55426

Phone: (612) 797-7464
Fax: (612) 797-9555
E-mail: ringjbrish@aol.com

JEFFREY B. RING: Mr. Ring practices exclusively in criminal defense litigation, with a strong focus on drunk driving defense and license revocation proceedings. A frequent lecturer for legal education DWI seminars, Mr. Ring was a prosecutor for nine years before committing the past eleven years to defense. He has successfully defended literally hundreds of drivers and has been able to reverse a high percentage of license revocations on varied grounds. He has secured several appellate decisions in his clients' favor, and has forged landmark law in the area of denial of access to an attorney before submitting to chemical testing. He is 1997 president of the Minnesota Society of Criminal Justice, an organization that annually hosts the nation's largest drunk driving defense seminar, and is past president of the Minnesota Family Support and Recovery Council. He has presented a number of workshops on DWI law and provides (through himself or an associate) 24-hour service, offering advice to drivers arrested and asked to submit to testing. Mr. Ring's advice in this area is widely sought after by his peers.

Education: JD 1977, University of Minnesota; BA 1973, University of Minnesota.

Admitted: 1977 Minnesota; 1977 U.S. Dist. Ct. (MN).

Employment History: Self-Employed Attorney 1993-present, Jeffrey B. Ring & Associates; Associate Attorney 1987-93, Allan H. Caplan & Associates; Assistant County Attorney 1979-87, Freeborn County; Law Clerk 1977-79, Hennepin County Attorney.

Professional Associations: Minnesota Society for Criminal Justice (President 1997); Minnesota Family Support and Recovery Counsel (President 1986).

Extensive Experience In:
- Criminal Litigation
- Drunk Driving Defense
- License Revocation Proceedings

FELONY & MISDEMEANOR CRIMINAL DEFENSE

Segal & Roston
250 Second Avenue South
Suite 225
Minneapolis, MN 55401
Phone: (612) 332-3100
Fax: (612) 335-3578

DAVID G. ROSTON

DAVID G. ROSTON: Mr. Roston has successfully defended and personally tried cases ranging from first degree murder to criminal misdemeanors, including high-profile matters involving public officials. He has extensive appellate experience, having written briefs and argued many cases in the Minnesota appellate courts and the Eighth Circuit Court of Appeals. Mr. Roston is coauthor (with Henry W. McCarr, Jr.) of *Minnesota Criminal Law and Procedure,* 1972, 1974. These books preceeded *Criminal Law and Procedure,* Minnesota Practice, volumes 7, 8 and 9, by Henry W. McCarr, Jr.

Education: JD 1969, University of Minnesota; BA 1967, University of Minnesota.

Admitted: 1970 Minnesota; 1972 U.S. Dist. Ct. (MN); 1973 U.S. Ct. App. (8th Cir.); 1973 U.S. Sup. Ct.

Employment History: Partner 1973-present, Segal & Roston; Assistant Attorney 1970-73, Hennepin County.

Professional Associations: National District Attorneys Assn. 1970-72; Minnesota Assn. of Criminal Defense Lawyers 1990-present.

Community Involvement: Intervention Institute (Advisory Board 1992-present).

Firm: Segal & Roston has been a partnership between David G. Roston and Allan E. Segal since 1974. Prior to that, both Mr. Roston and Mr. Segal were assistant Hennepin County attorneys in the appellate and criminal divisions. The firm represents clients in state and federal court and both partners have extensive trial experience. *See complete firm profile in the Firm Profiles section.*

FELONY & MISDEMEANOR CRIMINAL DEFENSE

Meshbesher & Spence, Ltd.
1616 Park Avenue South
Minneapolis, MN 55404

Phone: (612) 339-9121
Fax: (612) 339-9188
800: (800) 274-1616

JOHN P. SHEEHY

JOHN P. SHEEHY: Mr. Sheehy has concentrated his practice on criminal defense and civil trial work ranging from civil rights to medical malpractice. He has successfully tried dozens of jury trials in both criminal and civil areas including murder, assault, theft, conspiracy, drug distribution, criminal sexual conduct, police brutality and medical malpractice.

Education: JD 1984 cum laude, University of Minnesota; BA 1981, University of Minnesota.

Admitted: 1984 Minnesota; 1984 U.S. Ct. App. (8th Cir.).

Employment History: 1982-present, Meshbesher & Spence, Ltd.

Representative Clients: Mr. Sheehy represents various clients.

Professional Associations: NACDL; Minnesota Assn. of Criminal Defense Lawyers; ATLA; MTLA.

Firm: Meshbesher & Spence, Ltd., has a six-person criminal defense department, with Ronald Meshbesher as its head lawyer. The firm's lawyers have a wide variety of experience and skills in many areas of law. The firm is oriented toward trial work and litigation. *See complete firm profile in the Firm Profiles section.*

Extensive Experience In:
• Civil Trial

FELONY & MISDEMEANOR CRIMINAL DEFENSE

Law Offices of Thomas H. Shiah, Ltd.
701 Fourth Avenue South
Suite 1240
Minneapolis, MN 55415

Phone: (612) 338-0066
Fax: (612) 337-9020
E-mail: shiah@skypoint.com

THOMAS H. SHIAH

THOMAS H. SHIAH: Mr. Shiah's firm is engaged in criminal and civil practice in state and federal courts. The specific areas of practice are criminal, personal injury and family law matters. Mr. Shiah's primary practice is criminal law and he has represented defendants in a variety of cases including murder, narcotics, assault, racketeering, tax fraud, wire fraud, money laundering, gambling, DWI and sexual misconduct. He welcomes all referrals and telephone inquiries.

Education: JD 1973, St. John's University, New York; BA 1970, Niagara University.
Admitted: 1977 Minnesota; 1974 New York.
Employment History: 1974-present, Law Offices of Thomas H. Shiah, Ltd.
Representative Clients: The firm represents a variety of individuals involved in criminal, personal injury and family law matters.
Professional Associations: HCBA; NACDL; Minnesota Assn. of Criminal Defense Lawyers; Minnesota Society for Criminal Justice.
Firm: The Law Offices of Thomas H. Shiah, Ltd., is engaged in civil and criminal litigation. Mr. Shiah concentrates in criminal law but still represents a variety of individuals in personal injury and family law matters. In addition, he has represented Pfizer Inc., in a variety of matters over the past 20 years, including products liability and antitrust litigation in Minnesota. Cory D. Gilmer is also with the firm and he concentrates in divorce and personal injury law.

Extensive Experience In:
• Federal Trials
• State Trials
• Antitrust Litigation

FELONY & MISDEMEANOR CRIMINAL DEFENSE

Thorwaldsen, Quam, Beeson, Malmstrom & Sorum
1105 Highway 10 East
P.O. Box 1599
Detroit Lakes, MN 56502-1599

Phone: (218) 847-5646
Fax: (218) 847-3950

PAUL R.
THORWALDSEN

PAUL R. THORWALDSEN: With more than 20 years of experience, Mr. Thorwaldsen focuses his practice on plaintiffs' personal injury cases, wrongful death, products liability and employment claims, as well as criminal defense and divorce. He is a no-fault arbitrator for the American Arbitration Association and is active in alternative dispute resolution as a mediator and arbitrator.

Education: JD 1976, University of North Dakota; MS 1971, Moorhead State University; BS 1968, Moorhead State University.

Admitted: 1976 Minnesota.

Employment History: 1984-present, Thorwaldsen, Quam, Beeson, Malmstrom & Sorum; 1978-84, Wilson, Thorwaldsen & Shoemaker; 1976-78, Schroeder, Wilson, Thorwaldsen & Schroeder.

Representative Clients: Mr. Thorwaldsen represents individuals charged with criminal activities.

Professional Associations: MTLA; ATLA; ABA; Becker County Assn. (past President); Minnesota Assn. of Criminal Defense Lawyers; American Arbitration Assn. (Panel of Arbitrators); Minnesota Supreme Court (Panel of Arbitrators).

Community Involvement: Minnesota Duck Hunters Assn. [Smoky Hills Chapter (past President)]; El Zagal Shrine Color Guard (past President); Safari Club International (Great Plains Area Chapter); Ducks Unlimited; Rocky Mountain Elk Foundation.

Firm: Thorwaldsen, Quam, Beeson, Malmstrom & Sorum is a seven-person law firm. Three lawyers, including Mary Sorum—a lawyer and registered nurse—practice in plaintiffs' personal injury law. Five lawyers practice in criminal defense law. Brant Beeson is a Certified Real Estate Specialist who is also involved in commercial litigation. Carl Malmstrom practices in the areas of UCC, corporations and debtor/creditor relationships. Four attorneys also practice in family law. The firm represents several financial institutions, members of the Minnesota Education Association, several automobile dealerships and numerous other businesses. *See complete firm profile in the Firm Profiles section*

Extensive Experience In:
• DUI
• Property Crimes

FELONY & MISDEMEANOR CRIMINAL DEFENSE

Undem Law Office
521 North Pokegama Avenue
P.O. Box 428
Grand Rapids, MN 55744

Phone: (218) 326-0321
Fax: (218) 326-0248
E-mail: undem@northernnet.com

JOHN DRAKE
UNDEM

JOHN DRAKE UNDEM: Mr. Undem is a trial lawyer with extensive experience in criminal trials and personal injury law. Mr. Undem has successfully handled and tried every type of criminal case imaginable, including DWI, narcotics, armed robbery, sexual assault, battery and murder. He has successfully represented hundreds of people (or their families) who have been injured, maimed or killed because of defective products, automobile accidents, train accidents, airplane accidents or sexual abuse. Mr. Undem has taught and lectured on criminal and civil litigation and evidence at the college and law school level.

Education: JD 1984 with distinction, University of North Dakota (Order of the Coif); BA 1981 magna cum laude, Moorhead State University.

Admitted: 1984 Minnesota; 1986 U.S. Dist. Ct. (MN).

Employment History: 1996-present, Undem Law Office; 1987-96, Maturi & Undem; 1984-87, Shermoen, LeDuc & Jaksa; 1982-84, Grand Forks State's Attorney's Office.

Representative Clients: Mr. Undem represents individuals accused of crimes, and people (as well as their families) who have been injured or killed in automobile, airplane, products liability, medical malpractice and other negligence or personal injury actions.

Professional Associations: MSBA; MTLA; ATLA; Minnesota Assn. of Criminal Defense Lawyers.

Firm: Mr. Undem cofounded the Maturi & Undem law firm with Jon A. Maturi in Grand Rapids, Minnesota in 1987. Both Mr. Maturi and Mr. Undem brought extensive litigation experience to the firm. They served the citizens of northern Minnesota in criminal defense and personal injury matters until 1996, when Mr. Maturi became a judge. Today, Mr. Undem continues his practice as Undem Law Office at the same Grand Rapids location. The firm continues to successfully handle criminal and personal injury cases throughout northern Minnesota. In addition to Mr. Undem, the firm consists of an associate attorney and three highly trained staff. The firm is known for its professionalism and case preparation. Many of the firm's clients are direct referrals from other attorneys who do not practice in criminal defense or personal injury law. These attorneys have absolute confidence that their clients will receive expert representation from Undem Law Office.

FELONY & MISDEMEANOR CRIMINAL DEFENSE

Philip G. Villaume & Associates
7900 International Drive
Suite 675
Bloomington, MN 55425

Phone: (612) 851-0823
Fax: (612) 851-0824

PHILIP G.
VILLAUME

PHILIP G. VILLAUME: Mr. Villaume practices criminal defense law in state, federal and appellate courts. He has represented more than 500 professionals since 1986, including 400 educators. He defends law enforcement personnel accused of employment-related misconduct. He lectures and conducts workshops throughout the country on the prevention of workplace violence and harassment and is considered a national expert and consultant on topics of professional misconduct, harassment and violence in schools and in the workplace. Mr. Villaume was awarded a Certificate of Excellence in 1990 from Hamline University School of Law and the Judges Choice Award, Most Well-Prepared Lawyer in 1991. He is an adjunct professor for the University of Minnesota and University of St. Thomas and is the Course Chair and lecturer on criminal law, trial skills and employment law for Minnesota Continuing Legal Education. Mr. Villaume is the author of *The Law & Procedure Handbook for Minnesota Educators,* 1990; *The Better Work Environment,* 1997; and a coauthor of *Teachers At Risk,* 1993.

Education: JD 1979, Hamline University; BA 1971 magna cum laude, Macalester College.

Admitted: 1979 Minnesota; 1984 Wisconsin; 1984 U.S. Sup. Ct.

Employment History: 1979-present, Philip G. Villaume and Associates; Legal Investigator 1977-79, Villaume Investigative Services; Probation Officer 1972-76, Ramsey County Department of Community Corrections.

Representative Clients: Mr. Villaume represents educators, law enforcement officers, clergy, lawyers, physicians and other health care providers, business executives, corporations, educational institutions, professional associations and labor organizations including the Minnesota Police and Peace Officers Association and the Minnesota Federation of Teachers.

Professional Associations: MSBA; HCBA.

Firm: Founded in 1979, Philip G. Villaume and Associates, has been providing legal services to professionals and organizations for the past 18 years. Mr. Villaume is a national leader in representing professionals accused of employment-related misconduct. He and his two associates have handled several of Minnesota's high-profile cases involving allegations of professional misconduct since 1985. In 1986, the law firm successfully defended the leading teacher rights case in the country, *State v. Gruhl*; and in 1990, a precedent-setting case before the Supreme Court involving religious freedom with respect to the Amish and the slow-moving vehicle emblem, *State v. Hershberger*. The firm also provides pro bono legal service to the Amish communities in Minnesota and Wisconsin. In 1996, the firm successfully handled the precedent-setting case, *York v. Wood*, that involved workplace harassment of a public school teacher by a parent.

FELONY & MISDEMEANOR CRIMINAL DEFENSE

Wernick Law Office
2520 Park Avenue South
Minneapolis, MN 55404

Phone: (612) 871-8456
Fax: (612) 871-4168

MARK S. WERNICK

MARK S. WERNICK: With a criminal trial and appellate practice in federal and state courts, Mr. Wernick represents individuals either under investigation for or charged with white collar offenses, controlled substance offenses, homicide and other felony and misdemeanor offenses. He also represents businesses before various licensing authorities. One of his distinctions is having argued before the United States Supreme Court in *Minnesota v. Murphy* (probation officer need not give *Miranda* warnings to murder suspect during noncustodial interrogation). Mr. Wernick is Certified as a Criminal Trial Specialist by the National Board of Trial Advocacy. He is also the author of "Money Laundering: Let the Seller Beware," 61 *Hennepin Lawyer,* No. 2, 1991; and a lecturer for Minnesota Continuing Legal Education criminal law seminars on topics such as "Brainstorming for Themes and Theories of Defense for Federal Criminal Cases"; "In Defense of White Collar Crimes"; "Discovery in Complex Criminal Cases"; "Legal Fees, Money Laundering, and Forfeiture"; "Bail and Pretrial Detention Issues", "Immigration Consequences in Criminal Law"; and "Recent Cases—Search and Seizure."

Education: JD 1975 with honors, Drake University (Order of the Coif); BA 1972, University of Minnesota.

Admitted: 1975 Minnesota; 1976 U.S. Dist. Ct. (MN); 1978 U.S. Ct. App. (8th Cir.); 1982 U.S. Sup. Ct.; 1985 U.S. Tax Ct.

Employment History: Private Practice, 1977-present; Assistant Hennepin County Public Defender 1975-77.

Representative Clients: Mr. Wernick represents individuals and businesses who are either under investigation for or accused of criminal conduct.

Professional Associations: Academy of Certified Trial Lawyers of Minnesota; Minnesota Assn. of Criminal Defense Lawyers (Board of Directors 1996-97); NACDL; HCBA [Criminal Law Section (Cochair 1991-93)]; MSBA [Criminal Law Section (Chair 1994-95)].

Community Involvement: Legal Rights Center (President 1996-97; Board of Directors 1996-97); Sabathani Community Center (Board of Directors 1984-97); Minneapolis Civilian Review Working Committee—advisory committee to Minneapolis City Council regarding civilian review of police misconduct (Chair 1989).

Firm: Since leaving the Hennepin County Public Defender's Office in 1977, Mr. Wernick has been self-employed, practicing almost exclusively in criminal defense. While in private practice, Mr. Wernick has achieved an acquittal rate of over 70 percent in state court jury trials.

Extensive Experience In:
• White Collar Offenses
• Controlled Substance Offenses
• Homicide Offenses

BLETHEN, GAGE & KRAUSE, PLLP

127 South Second Street - P.O. Box 3049 - Mankato, MN 56002-3049
Phone: (507) 345-1166, Fax: (507) 345-8003

Blethen, Gage & Krause, PLLP, is a full-service law firm that has included among its ranks a former chief justice of the Minnesota Supreme Court, a past president of the MSBA and leaders in numerous civic and professional organizations.

One of the oldest and largest law firms in southern Minnesota, Blethen, Gage & Krause, PLLP, places special emphasis on civil litigation, including personal injury, products liability and insurance defense, as well as business and corporate law. The firm practices with a team approach, creating an in-depth body of knowledge and experience specific to each case. Clients are assured the highest level of service in all areas of law.

Since the firm's founding in 1896, its philosophy has demanded a strong commitment to professional excellence from its attorneys and encouraged participation in civic, educational, professional and public service.

Although Blethen, Gage & Krause, PLLP, has existed for many years, it is entirely contemporary in maintaining state-of-the-art technology necessary to efficient, cost-effective, high quality legal services.

The firm has 11 attorneys: **Kelton Gage, Bailey W. Blethen, Richard J. Corcoran, Randall C. Berklund** (also licensed to practice in Iowa), **David T. Peterson, James H. Turk** (Certified as a Civil Trial Specialist by the NBTA and MSBA), **Michael C. Karp** (CPA and MSBA Certified Real Property Law Specialist), **William David Taylor III, PhD., Julia Kethcam-Corbett, Silas L. Danielson** (CPA) and **Jeffrey D. Gednalske** (also licensed to practice in Iowa and South Dakota). Its support staff of paraprofessionals and legal secretaries is of the highest caliber.

During the nearly 100 years that Blethen, Gage & Krause, PLLP, has been a presence in southern Minnesota, the firm has always held to the highest professional and ethical standards and has supported the talent and financial endeavors of local businesses. This commitment to excellence was recognized in 1994 when Blethen, Gage & Krause, PLLP, was elected to the Mankato Area Business Hall of Fame.

MANAHAN & BLUTH LAW OFFICE, CHARTERED

416 South Front Street - P.O. Box 287 - Mankato, MN 56002-0287
Phone: (507) 387-5661, Fax: (507) 387-2111, E-mail: mb_law@ic.mankato.mn.us

Manahan & Bluth Law Office, Chartered, has engaged in the practice of law in the Mankato area since 1972. The firm emphasizes trial practice in both federal and state courts, and its members hold licenses in the state courts of Hawaii, Colorado, and Wisconsin as well as Minnesota. The owners, James H. Manahan and Joseph P. Bluth, handle both criminal and civil litigation, with emphasis in the areas of personal injury, civil rights, tort, employment, discrimination, environmental and family law. Both lawyers defend serious felony and DUI cases.

James Manahan is a member and former Dean of the Academy of Certified Trial Lawyers of Minnesota, a fellow and past president of the Minnesota Chapter of the American Academy of Matrimonial Lawyers, and a Diplomate of the American College of Family Trial Lawyers. He is listed in *The Best Lawyers in America* and Leading Minnesota Attorneys Guides to *Plaintiffs' Personal Injury Law, Family Law*, and *Criminal Defense Law*. He is an Arbitrator for the American Arbitration Association. Mr. Manahan is a reviewer of Minnesota Supreme Court and Court of Appeals family law decisions for the Minnesota Summary Reporter. He has handled 38 appeals to the state and federal appellate courts.

Joseph Bluth is a Fellow of the American Academy of Matrimonial Lawyers and president-elect of the Minnesota Chapter. He is a member of the Association of Trial Lawyers of America, the Minnesota Trial Lawyers Association, and the National Association of Criminal Defense Lawyers. He is on the Association of Trial Lawyers of America panel of experts and lecturers, and is a member and former president of the Minnesota Society for Criminal Justice. Mr. Bluth is listed in *Leading Minnesota Attorneys Guides to Family Law and Criminal Defense Law* and is listed in *The Best Lawyers in America*.

Mr. Manahan and Mr. Bluth are frequent speakers at national and international legal seminars and conferences. The firm members occasionally provide services as volunteer attorneys for cases sponsored by the Minnesota Civil Liberties Union as well as the Southern Minnesota Regional Legal Services. Over the past four years, Manahan & Bluth Law Office, Chartered, has funded and hosted five regional Continuing Legal Education programs. They have participated as speakers in numerous CLE courses and nonlegal programs throughout the state and nationally.

MESHBESHER & SPENCE, LTD.

1616 Park Avenue - Minneapolis, MN 55404
Phone: (612) 339-9121, Fax: (612) 339-9188

Meshbesher & Spence is a nationally recognized firm of trial lawyers specializing in civil and criminal law. President Ron Meshbesher was recognized as one of "Minnesota's Winningest Trial Lawyers" by *Minnesota Lawyer* in 1991.

Meshbesher & Spence, Ltd., has handled some of the largest and most significant state and national cases. They have served as co-lead counsel in the Dalkon Shield Class Action Settlement—one of the largest products liability settlements in United States history.

Meshbesher & Spence, Ltd., emphasizes that while it handles major cases, each individual case is treated as such and each individual client is treated as if his or her case is the most important one in the office.

Most clients choose Meshbesher & Spence, Ltd., based on the firm's reputation, past client referrals and individual lawyer contacts.

The firm's 26 lawyers are divided into three departments with a focus on litigation, trial work, mediation and dispute resolution:

1. The Personal Injury, Accident and Insurance Claims Group
2. The Criminal Defense, Traffic and Appellate Practice Group
3. The Business Practice Group

Each group provides quality legal services at five locations in Minnesota: Minneapolis, Minnetonka, Rochester, St. Cloud and Woodbury.

The branch offices and three departments are linked by computer and by fax and to the resources of a centralized library and a research and investigation database. A team of well-experienced lawyers and investigators offer complete legal services to the firm's clients.

Ron Meshbesher, Russ Spence and Dennis Johnson, all past Presidents of the Minnesota Trial Lawyers Association, lead a team of 15 lawyers in the accident and injury department. They've won thousands of settlements and verdicts in accident cases.

All accident and personal injury claims are handled on a contingent fee basis. This means there are no fees until the client collects. Fees in the other types of cases are reasonable and competitive.

Many legal problems can be resolved with a simple consultation. Meshbesher & Spence's lawyers explain a client's rights in advance so there are no surprises.

If it is difficult or impossible to meet in any of the office locations (where parking is always free), a lawyer will meet with you in your home, office or the hospital.

A 24-hour emergency service and evening and weekend appointments are available upon request.

Meshbesher & Spence, Ltd., was incorporated in 1977. The law firm previously functioned as a partnership, with its beginnings in 1961.

The firm's other offices are located in:

Minnetonka
601 Carlson Parkway
Suite 1500
Minnetonka, MN 55305
Phone: (612) 476-9941
Toll-Free: 1-800-274-1616
Fax: (612) 476-9937

St. Cloud
Zapp Bank Plaza
1015 St. Germain Street West
St. Cloud, MN 56301
Phone: (320) 656-0484
Toll-Free: 1-800-395-5297
Fax: (320) 656-0845

Rochester
21 South Second Street
Rochester, MN 55902
Phone: (507) 280-8090
Toll-Free:1-800-845-1021
Fax: (507) 280-0807

Woodbury
Valley Creek Professional Building
8360 City Centre Drive
Suite 100
Woodbury, MN 55125
Phone: (612) 578-8055
Toll-Free: 1-800-274-1616
Fax: (612) 578-8373

Ronald I. Meshbesher is a well-known trial lawyer with outstanding success in personal injury and criminal defense. He is the firm's president, the author of the *Trial Handbook for Minnesota Lawyers* and listed in *The Best Lawyers in America, Who's Who in American Law* and *Who's Who in the World*.

Russell M. Spence focuses primarily on trials and appeals, personal injury and products liability. He has been listed since 1987 in *The Best Lawyers in America* under "Best Lawyers in Minnesota." Mr. Spence is a frequent lecturer and is a past president of the Minnesota Trial Lawyers Association.

Dennis R. Johnson has practiced exclusively in personal injury, wrongful death, aviation accidents and products liability. A past President of the Minnesota Trial Lawyers Association, he co-leads a team of 15 lawyers in the firm's accident and injury department. He is a Certified Trial Litigation Specialist and a frequent lecturer.

Michael C. Snyder has extensive experience in appellate practice. He works exclusively in personal injury, products liability, wrongful death and insurance-related issues. He serves on the Minnesota Trial Lawyers Association's Amicus Curiae Committee and is Certified as an Arbitrator by the American Arbitration Association.

Jeffrey P. Oistad represents accident victims for personal injury claims. He has extensive experience in automobile accidents, premises liability and wrongful death. He has been the managing partner of the firm's St. Cloud office since its opening in 1991. Mr. Oistad has served on the firm's Board of Directors since 1996.

John Sheehy concentrates on criminal defense and civil trial work. He has successfully tried dozens of jury trials including murder, assault, theft, conspiracy, drug distribution, criminal sexual conduct, police brutality and medical malpractice. He is a member of the National and Minnesota Associations of Criminal Defense Lawyers.

SEGAL & ROSTON
250 Second Avenue South, Suite 225 - Minneapolis, MN 55401
Phone: (612) 332-3100, Fax: (612) 335-3578

David Roston and Alan Segal have been practicing law together continuously since 1973. Prior to their law firm's establishment, both were Assistant Hennepin County Attorneys for three years, prosecuting criminal felony trials and appeals to the Minnesota Supreme Court.

The firm has defended several high-profile cases including homicides, criminal actions involving public officials, and other celebrated cases. The firm successfully codefended a young mother accused of harming her young child because of the psychological condition "Munchausen Syndrome by Proxy."

Mr. Roston also represented a former public official accused of criminal misconduct and prosecuted by the attorney general's office after a local television station's undercover investigation. An order dismissing the indictment was upheld by the Minnesota Supreme Court.

Both Segal and Roston also enjoy representing indigent individuals in their capacity as part-time Hennepin County public defenders.

Alan Segal is a 1969 graduate of the University of Minnesota Law School. Prior to law school, he served in Vietnam as an officer in the United States Navy. He is a member of the National Association of Criminal Defense Attorneys and the Minnesota Association of Criminal Defense Attorneys.

David G. Roston is a 1969 graduate of the University of Minnesota Law School. He is a member of the Minnesota Association of Criminal Defense Attorneys.

THORNTON, HEGG, REIF, JOHNSTON & DOLAN, P.A.
1017 Broadway - P.O. Box 819 - Alexandria, MN 56308
Phone: (320) 762-2361, Fax: (320) 762-1638, E-mail: thrjd@alexandria.polaristcl.net

Thornton, Hegg, Reif, Johnston & Dolan, P.A., was founded in 1914 by Ralph S. Thornton. The firm is a general practice firm dedicated to providing quality legal services to individuals in greater Minnesota. Attorneys within the firm specialize in individual practice areas, thereby allowing clients to receive specialized legal services within one general practice law firm.

The attorneys of Thornton, Hegg, Reif, Johnston & Dolan, P.A., provide full service legal representation, including accident and personal injury; business and corporation; criminal law; divorce and adoption; elder law; estate planning; wills and trusts; probate; nursing home law; real estate and title insurance; and environmental law.

R. S. Thornton (1892-1960)

J. G. Thornton (1923-1996)

Thomas Reif (JD 1973, William Mitchell) practices in personal injury, products liability, contractual disputes, real estate controversies and domestic relations. He has provided meditation and arbitration services since 1990, and he is an arbitrator for the American Arbitration Association.

Michael J. Dolan: Mr. Dolan has been practicing criminal law since 1983 as an Assistant County Attorney, City Attorney, Special Prosecutor, Assistant State Public Defender and Assistant County Public Defender. He is Certified as a Civil Trial Specialist by the Minnesota State Bar Association.

Robert M. Hegg (JD 1970, University of Minnesota) is experienced in elder law, estate planning, probate law, real estate law and nursing home planning. He is a member of the American College of Trust and Estate Council and is a frequent CLE lecturer.

Scott T. Johnston (JD 1979, University of North Dakota) is a Real Property Specialist Certified by the Real Property Section of the Minnesota State Bar Association and practices in the areas of real estate law, corporate and banking law, and business formation. He is a recent recipient of the Vikingland Builders Association Associate of the Year.

Lisa J. Bowen (JD 1995 cum laude, Hamline University) worked for the Southern Minnesota Regional Legal Services from 1995 to 1996, representing class members in a complex class action housing discrimination suit. She currently practices in the areas of estate planning, wills, trusts and nursing home law.

The firm is committed to the proposition that quality legal services are best provided by hard work, aggressive but ethical representation, a commitment to individual clients and a willingness to try cases.

THORWALDSEN, QUAM, BEESON, MALMSTROM & SORUM

1105 Highway 10 East - P.O. Box 1599 - Detroit Lakes, MN 56502-1599
Phone: (218) 847-5646, Fax: (218) 847-3950

Thorwaldsen, Quam, Beeson, Malmstrom & Sorum is a seven-person law firm covering many areas of law. Five lawyers practice in criminal defense; three lawyers, including Mary Sorum, a lawyer and registered nurse, practice in plaintiff's personal injury. Five of its attorneys also practice in family law.

Brant R. Beeson (JD 1977, Hamline University) practices primarily in real estate law. He was Certified as a Real Estate Specialist by the Minnesota State Bar Association's Real Property Section in January 1991 and has also been a Title Agent for Chicago Title Insurance Company since 1981. He also practices in business and banking law, probate and corporations law. He is licensed in Minnesota and North Dakota state and federal courts.

Carl E. Malmstrom (JD 1982, Valparaiso University) engages in a general practice, working primarily in business and criminal litigation, real estate, family law, wills, probates and estates. Mr. Malmstrom is an agent for Attorneys' Title Guaranty Fund and is the Examiner of Titles for Becker County, Minnesota, for Torrens proceedings.

Mary G. Sorum (JD 1985, University of North Dakota) practices in family law, wills, estate planning, probate, personal injury and Social Security law. Ms. Sorum is a registered nurse and is licensed in Minnesota and North Dakota state courts.

John C. Quam (LLB 1964, University of North Dakota) focuses primarily on litigation, with more than 450 jury trials completed in criminal defense, business and contract, and personal injury law. These criminal and civil trials include trials in Minnesota and North Dakota federal and state district courts, with the majority in western Minnesota. He is also an Arbitrator for the American Arbitration Association.

Paul Thorwaldsen (JD 1976, University of North Dakota) practices criminal defense, personal injury (plaintiff) and divorce and family law, as well as business and civil litigation. He is also an Arbitrator for the American Arbitration Association and provides services as a Qualified ADR Neutral Civil and Family Law Mediator.

James W. Donehower (JD 1990, Vanderbilt University) engages in a broad litigation practice with particular emphasis in family law, restraining order practice and criminal defense. His extensive criminal defense includes more than five years of service as a county and district public defender. His professional associations include the American Bar Association, Minnesota State Bar Association and Becker County Bar Association, as well as a position on the Minnesota Public Defender's Association's Executive Committee.

Stuart J. Kitzmann (JD 1990, Hamline University) engages primarily in criminal defense, family law, employment and insurance law, as well as probates and estates, wills and workers' compensation. After obtaining his JD at Hamline University, Mr. Kitzmann was the judicial law clerk for the Honorable William E. Walker, Chief Judge of the Seventh Judicial District of the State of Minnesota.

IMMIGRATION LAW:
INDIVIDUAL

For centuries, people from around the world have been coming to the United States. They come to work, get an education, escape oppression, start a new life, do business, visit friends, or sightsee. Over the years, the United States has seen tremendous diversity in immigrants' nations of origins and their reasons for coming here. In response to the incredible demand for permission to enter this country, the federal government has established a complex set of laws that determines who may enter this country and for what reasons. This chapter discusses legal immigration and travel to the United States.

UNITED STATES CITIZENSHIP

United States citizens have a right to travel to and live in the United States and enjoy the fullest protection of its laws. People who are not citizens of the United States usually must have a visa to enter and may not enjoy the protection of all laws.

A person can become a United States citizen either through birth or through a process known as naturalization. A person can be a citizen from birth either by being born here or by being born in a foreign country to a parent who is a citizen of the United States. Anyone born in the United States has automatic citizenship, regardless of the parents' citizenship, and even if both parents are living in this country illegally at the time of the child's birth. The only exception is that children born to foreign diplomats in the United States do not get automatic citizenship. Anyone not born a citizen must be naturalized to become a citizen. Occasionally, a group of people is naturalized by treaty or by act of Congress. Usually, a person goes through the process individually.

ALIENS, IMMIGRANTS, NONIMMIGRANTS AND RESIDENTS

An alien is a citizen of any country other than the United States. A person who comes here to stay permanently is called an immigrant. Someone who intends to return to his or her country of origin is called a nonimmigrant, even if he or she intends to stay for a substantial period of time. For example, a student might stay in the United States many years to complete an education and still be considered a nonimmigrant. The distinction between immigrant and nonimmigrant is crucial. Permission to enter as a nonimmigrant often is easier to get than permission to enter as an immigrant, so some people are tempted to claim they intend to return to their home country in order to enter this country. The Immigration and Naturalization Service (INS) is aware of this temptation and often will deny a nonimmigrant visa application to anyone suspected of wanting to remain permanently. Also, being granted a nonimmigrant visa sometimes can make it more difficult to get an immigrant visa later. A permanent resident is an alien who has been given permission to live permanently in the United States.

In a dispute with the INS over an applicant's true intent, the applicant always bears the burden of proving intent to remain here temporarily. For some people, this burden is nearly impossible to overcome. For example, the spouse of a permanent resident normally must wait over two years for available immigrant visas. If he or she claims to want to visit only temporarily, he or she must overcome the presumption that a married person would want to remain permanently with his or her spouse.

THE VISA SYSTEM

A visa is a stamp in a person's passport that gives him or her conditional approval to enter the United States. Most matters involving visas are handled by the INS. Most aliens apply for visas from a consulate or embassy of the United States in their home countries.

Citizens of some countries, primarily European countries and Japan, may enter the United States for up to 90 days without a visa. To be eligible, countries' citizens must show the INS that they have a return ticket home and that they intend to engage in a type of business or tourist activity that would be allowed under a "B Visa," described below. Canadian citizens generally do not need visas to enter temporarily. In some instances, they must obtain INS approval in advance if they are coming here to work.

Congress establishes a complex set of quotas that limits the number of visas that can be granted for most types of visas. Whether an applicant receives a visa turns on the type of visa requested, the applicant's reason for traveling to the United States and the applicant's country of origin. Probably the most important element to obtaining a visa successfully is knowing for which visa category to apply. For certain categories of visas and certain countries of origin, an applicant can wait many years before he or she even will be considered for a visa. Sometimes the wait would be much shorter if the applicant applied for a different type of visa. Unfortunately, once an applicant applies for one type of visa, it can be difficult to change the application to another class of visa. For this reason, it is wise to consult an immigration attorney before applying for any kind of visa.

NONIMMIGRANT VISAS

There are different kinds of nonimmigrant visas, identified by the letters A–R, available for persons who do not intend to remain in the United States permanently. All nonimmigrant visas are based on what the applicant intends to do in this country. It is important that employers be aware of the variety of visas that exist. Following is a list of the categories of visas available.

A Visas: for diplomats and their families.

B Visas: for aliens coming to this country to do business but not for employment or labor for hire, such as to do business research, engage in litigation, or negotiate contracts; B-2 Visas, the most common nonimmigrant visas, allow aliens to enter the country temporarily to engage in tourism, visit with friends or relatives or to receive medical treatment.

C Visas: to enter the United States only for immediate and continuous transit through the country to a third country.

D Visas: for crew members of foreign vessels or airplanes.

E Visas: for traders and investors covered by commercial treaties between the United States and foreign countries, as well as spouses and children of E Visa holders.

F Visas: for students in full-time academic programs, from the elementary school level up to the post-graduate level, as well as spouses and children of F Visa holders, and allowing employment for fewer than 20 hours a week, mainly at certain on-campus jobs typically done by students.

G Visas: for representatives, officers and employees of foreign countries to international organizations.

H Visas: for workers needed by U.S. employers to fill temporary openings; H-1B Visas are commonly held by aliens with highly specialized knowledge working in professional jobs.

I Visas: for media representatives and their families.

J Visas: designed to bring foreigners here to participate in exchange programs designated by the United States Information Agency.

K Visas: to allow an alien engaged to a United States citizen to enter to marry the citizen, as well as for any minor children of the alien.

L Visas: for intracompany employee transfers (e.g., for employees of multinational corporations).

M Visas: for students in vocational or nonacademic study programs.

N Visas: for relatives of certain international organization employees here on G Visas.

O Visas: for artists, entertainers, athletes, scientists and certain business professionals with extraordinary ability in their field, and persons needed to accompany and assist them.

P Visas: for performing artists, entertainers and athletes; similar to O Visas, but easier to get and intended more for group entertainers or athletes who come here for a specific performance or tour.

Q Visas: for participants in international cultural exchanges.

R Visas: for religious workers and their families.

IMMIGRANT VISAS
An applicant who intends to stay in this country permanently generally is admitted either on the basis of employment or family connections. The main exception is for political asylum seekers.

Employment-Based Immigration
An alien can receive permission to immigrate to this country on the basis of his or her employment. There are five categories of employment, known as preferences, through which an alien can be permitted to immigrate.

First Preference: Individuals of extraordinary ability, outstanding professors or researchers, and multinational executives.

Second Preference: Professionals with advanced degrees and aliens with exceptional abilities in science, art or business. (Note: The terminology is confusing, but "exceptional ability" is a different standard from "extraordinary ability.")

Third Preference: Skilled workers, professionals and other workers for which there is a shortage of workers in the United States.

Fourth Preference: Certain special workers, such as religious workers.

Fifth Preference: Investors creating employment for workers in the United States. The investment must be substantial (i.e., between $500,000 and $1,000,000).

Family-Based Immigration
An alien can get a visa as an immediate relative of a United States citizen if he or she is the citizen's child, spouse or parent. In addition, there are four family-based immigrant visa categories:

First Preference: Unmarried children of United States citizens.

Second Preference: Spouses and unmarried children of lawful permanent residents.

Third Preference: Married children of United States citizens.

Fourth Preference: Siblings of adult United States citizens.

Each preference is allotted a total number of visas. Generally speaking, the higher the applicant's preference, the shorter the wait to get a visa.

Special Classes of Immigrants
Some groups of immigrants receive special treatment and fall outside the preference system described above.

Diversity immigrants are immigrants from countries deemed under-represented in the applicant pool for visas throughout the years. A new program implemented by the INS in 1995 provides a certain number of visas to be granted to applicants from low-admission countries. Applicants also must have a high school education or two years of training or experience in a particular occupation.

A person is a refugee if he or she is outside the United States, is fleeing or has fled his or her country, and has a well-founded fear that if returned to the home country, he or she will be persecuted because of race, religion, nationality, membership in a particular social group, or political opinion. An asylee is an alien already in the United States who, like a refugee, has a well-founded fear of persecution if returned to his or her home country. The President and Congress decide each year the total number of refugees and asylees to accept into the country. Occasionally, Congress grants immigrant visas allotted for individuals from specific countries according to political factors. Recent programs have included China, Hong Kong and Tibet.

ENTRY AND EXCLUSION
A visa only gives conditional approval to enter the country. Once an alien arrives in the United States with a visa, he or she must apply for entry from INS officials at the point of entry. For most aliens, this is a mere formality, but INS can exclude persons with valid

visas for a variety of reasons including communicable diseases, physical or mental disorders that pose a threat to others, drug addiction or criminal history. Involvement in espionage or terrorist activity against the United States government or its people is grounds for exclusion. The Secretary of State also has broad discretion to bar entry of anyone whose presence would have an adverse effect on the foreign policy of the United States. Sometimes, waivers are available for aliens who otherwise would be denied entry for certain reasons. For example, the child of a United States citizen may be granted a waiver to enter to receive treatment for drug addiction.

GETTING A GREEN CARD AND BECOMING A NATURALIZED CITIZEN

Becoming a permanent resident is the first step that an alien must take to become a naturalized American citizen. People with permission to live in the United States permanently are issued "green cards" that allow them to work with few restrictions. A permanent resident can apply to become a naturalized citizen after five years, or three years if married to a United States citizen.

The INS is diligent in investigating marriages between United States citizens and aliens to ensure that aliens do not become permanent residents through sham marriages. Immigration law specifies that an alien seeking permanent residence based on a marriage to a United States citizen of less than two years first is granted conditional permanent resident status. After two years, the husband and wife must apply to the INS to remove this conditional status.

DEPORTATION

Deportation is the expulsion of an alien who entered illegally, or entered legally but has done something to become deportable. With few exceptions, any violation of the conditions of a visa, no matter how minor, is grounds for deportation to a person's country of origin. Conviction for any crime but the most minor also is grounds for deportation. Deportation can delay an alien whose long-term goal is to live permanently in this country. After being deported, aliens are forbidden to re-enter the country for five years. Aliens deported for aggravated felonies, such as drug smuggling, are barred from re-entry for 20 years or may be barred permanently. The delay in returning to the United States may be even greater for aliens from countries with long waiting lists. Returning home under a deportation order may result in the embassy's refusal to entrust the individual with another temporary visa.

There are a number of remedies to deportation, especially if the deportable person has lived in the United States for a long time, building a life that demonstrates good moral character. Even if the deportable individual has not been here long, there may be certain waivers or defenses to deportation. Among the most common is asking the court for "voluntary departure," which allows the individual to depart the United States on his or her own. In any case, anyone facing deportation should seek the advice of counsel well in advance of a deportation hearing.

IMMIGRATION LAW: INDIVIDUAL

Borene Law Firm, P.A.
Immigration Law Group
4602 IDS Center
Minneapolis, MN 55402

Phone: (612) 321-0082
Fax: (612) 332-8368

SCOTT M. BORENE

SCOTT M. BORENE: Mr. Borene leads the Borene Law Firm's Immigration Law Group. Since establishing his practice in 1979, he has had 18 years of experience handling immigration casework concentrating on employment-based and corporate immigration matters. In 1996, Mr. Borene was selected as chair of the American Immigration Lawyers Association National Conference, the world's largest immigration law conference. Mr. Borene is a past member of the American Immigration Lawyers Association's (AILA) National Board of Governors and a past Chair for the Minnesota/Dakotas Region. He is currently vice chair of the Immigration Law Committee of the American Bar Association's International Law Section. In 1995, he served as editor of AILA's reference publication, *INS Forms for Applications and Petitions* (3rd edition). Since 1993, he has been invited as a speaker at all AILA National Conferences. In 1994, he spoke on Priority Workers; in 1995, he spoke on Medical Personnel; and in 1996, he chaired the session on "Going Global: Temporary WorkPermit/Visa Options Around the World."

Education: JD 1978, William Mitchell; AB 1971, Harvard University (National Merit Scholar).

Admitted: 1979 Minnesota; 1979 U.S. Dist. Ct. (MN).

Representative Clients: Clients include the Mayo Clinic; Mayo Foundation; Medtronic Corporation; GMAC/Residential Funding Corporation; the University of Minnesota; ACT/American College Testing; Saint Paul Pioneer Press; Schwing America; Schneider National; Harmon Contract; Luther College; North Dakota State University; Ihle Orthopedic Clinic; DataMedica; and Richfield Bank and Trust.

Professional Associations: American Immigration Lawyers Association—AILA [1996 National Conference Program (Chair); National Board of Governors 1992-94; Minnesota/Dakotas Region (Chair 1992-94)]; ABA [International Section (Immigration Committee, National Vice Chair 1995-present)]; International Bar Assn. [Immigration Committee (National Representative for the United States 1994-present)].

Community Involvement: Minnesota Advocates for Human Rights (Volunteer-Instructor); Harvard/Radcliffe Club of Minnesota (Executive Committee).

Firm: Borene Law Firm, P.A., handles permanent employment-based immigration, temporary visas and work permits for clients from every region of the world and more than 125 countries. Business clients include Fortune 500 companies, international law firms, investors, major hospitals and research universities, family-owned and small businesses and entrepreneurs. Professional clients include business executives and managers, scientific and technical professionals, physicians, researchers, computer and engineering professionals, educators, prominent public figures, artists, entertainers, athletes and skilled workers.

Extensive Experience In:
• Visas
• Work Permits
• Employment-based Immigration

IMMIGRATION LAW: INDIVIDUAL

LAURA J. DANIELSON

Patterson & Keough, P.A.
1200 Rand Tower
527 Marquette Avenue South
Minneapolis, MN 55402

Phone: (612) 349-5767
Fax: (612) 349-9266
800: (800) 331-4537
E-mail: 1jd@pklaw.com

LAURA J. DANIELSON: Ms. Danielson represents clients in immigration matters with special emphasis on arts and business-related immigration. She represents foreign artists, entertainers, athletes, engineers, scientists, medical personnel and other professionals in nonimmigrant and immigrant visa matters. Ms. Danielson handles numerous cases for individuals with exceptional talent or whose work is in the national interest. She also takes cases involving family immigration and political asylum. She teaches immigration law at the University of Minnesota School of Law and has lectured on immigration topics at national conferences across the United States. She is a former legal writing instructor at William Mitchell and the University of Minnesota Law Schools and has written numerous articles for publication by the American Immigration Lawyers Association.

Education: JD 1989 cum laude, University of Minnesota; BA 1977, Carleton College.

Admitted: 1989 Minnesota; 1994 U.S. Dist. Ct. (MN).

Employment History: Attorney/Officer 1994-present, Patterson & Keough, P.A.; Partner 1991-1994, Danielson & Begley, P.A.; Attorney 1989-91, John M. Roth & Associates.

Representative Clients: Ms. Danielson represents numerous businesses, arts organizations and individuals.

Professional Associations: Minnesota Advocates for Human Rights (Board of Directors 1996-present); American Immigration Lawyers Assn. 1989-present.

Community Involvement: Minnesota Advocates for Human Rights (Pro Bono Asylum Attorney); Southern Theatre (Board Member 1991-present).

Firm: Patterson & Keough, P.A., provides services in intellectual property, representing clients in the areas of copyrights, trademarks, patents, trade secrets, related litigation, licensing and immigration. The firm serves a broad spectrum of clients ranging from creative individuals to Fortune 500 companies. Since its inception in 1991, Patterson & Keough, P.A.'s practice has focused on meeting the needs of a full range of intellectual property clients—from inventors and engineers to artists and entertainers.

Extensive Experience In:
• National Interest Waivers
• Outstanding Researchers
• Arts Immigration

Attorney at Law
Rowan Professional Building
1539 Grand Avenue
St. Paul, MN 55105

Phone: (612) 698-8841
Fax: (612) 698-5703

PATRICIA G.
MATTOS

PATRICIA G. MATTOS: Ms. Mattos has experience in all areas of family-based immigration, including petitions by spouses, parents and children. She has worked extensively with clients in helping to get family members to the United States. Her expertise includes all areas of naturalization and assessment of possible claims to United States citizenship through parents. Ms. Mattos works with individuals seeking H and L visas, E trader and investor nonimmigrants, individuals with J exchange visitor visas subject to a two-year foreign residency requirement, individuals applying for labor certification, and college and university professors seeking to immigrate on the basis of their professions. She works with individuals seeking employment creation immigrant visas, aliens of extraordinary ability, and represents individuals applying for asylum and seeking to immigrate as religious workers. Ms. Mattos' experience also includes working with corporate clients in transferring managers and executives to the United States under L-1 nonimmigrant visas and obtaining subsequent permanent resident status for these clients. She works with corporations seeking labor certification for employees and with subsequent applications for permanent resident status. She is a frequent lecturer on immigration and asylum law for the Minnesota Institute for Legal Education and Minnesota Advocates for Human Rights. She has also been a guest lecturer at Hamline University School of Law.

Education JD 1982, William Mitchell; BA 1976, Augsburg College.

Admitted: 1982 Minnesota; 1982 U.S. Dist. Ct. (MN); 1983 U.S. Ct. App. (8th Cir.).

Employment History: Private Practice 1982-present; Law Clerk 1981-82, Robins Kaplan Miller & Ciresi; Legal Assistant 1979-81, Dorsey & Whitney.

Professional Associations: MSBA [Immigration Section (past Chair 1988-90)]; American Immigration Lawyers Assn. (past Secretary/Treasurer 1990-91); Minnesota Dakotas Chapter.

Community Involvement: Minnesota Advocates for Human Rights [Pro Bono Asylum Project (Consulting Lawyer)]; MSBA/American Immigration Lawyers Assn. [Pro Bono Master Calendar Project (Volunteer Attorney)].

Firm: Ms. Mattos is a sole practioner in St. Paul and has worked exclusively in immigration and naturalization law since 1982. She has developed expertise in all facets of immigration practice and successfully represents clients at every stage of proceedings.

Immigration Law: Individual

Borene Law Firm, P.A.
Immigration Law Group
4602 IDS Center
Minneapolis, MN 55402

Phone: (612) 321-0082
Fax: (612) 332-8368

Saiko Y. McIvor

SAIKO Y. MC IVOR: Ms. McIvor has ten years of experience in immigration law practice, with emphasis on employment-related immigration cases. Prior to limiting her practice exclusively to immigration law, Ms. McIvor practiced extensively in international, corporate, employment and health care law, representing primarily Fortune 500 companies and mega-scaled health care organizations. Educated both in the United States and Japan, she has also developed an expertise in corporate development and negotiations with Japanese corporations, and played a major role in the development of United States corporations and governmental entities (e.g. State of Minnesota) in the Asian market. Ms. McIvor continues to represent such organizations in immigration law. She was chair of the Minnesota State Bar Association's Immigration Law Section from 1994 to 1996 and is a frequent lecturer at various professional and academic forums including the Minnesota Institute of Legal Education and the University of Minnesota Law School. Her publications include "Step-by-Step Guide for Labor Certification" and "Immigrant Workers and Anti-Immigrant Sentiment Today." Recently, Ms. McIvor was profiled by Asahi Newspaper as a Most Influential Professional in Immigration Law.

Education: JD 1984, Golden Gate University, San Francisco; BS 1976, University of Washington.

Admitted: 1987 Minnesota; 1987 U.S. Ct. of International Trade.

Employment History: Attorney 1991-present, Borene Law Firm, P.A.; Attorney 1987-90, Dorsey & Whitney; Law Clerk 1983-84, Werner & Allen & Associates, San Francisco.

Representative Clients: Ms. McIvor represents major organizations, law firms and their employees (including the Mayo Foundation, Medtronic Corp., and the University of Minnesota) in both the private and public sectors.

Professional Associations: MSBA [Immigration Law Section (Chair 1994-95, 1995-96); International Law Section]; American Immigration Lawyers Assn.

Community Involvement: Japan-America Society of Minnesota; City of St. Louis Park (Human Rights Committee); Edina and St. Louis Park School Districts (Volunteer).

Firm: Borene Law Firm, P.A., handles permanent employment-based immigration, temporary visas and work permits for clients from every region of the world and more than 125 countries. Business clients include Fortune 500 companies, international law firms, investors, major hospitals and research universities, family-owned and small businesses, and entrepreneurs. Professional clients include business executives and managers, scientific and technical professionals, physicians, researchers, computer and engineering professionals, educators, prominent public figures, artists, entertainers, athletes and skilled workers. *See complete firm profile in the Firm Profiles section.*

Extensive Experience In:
- Employment-Based Immigration
- Corporate/Engineering Visas
- Scientific/Health Care Visas

BORENE LAW FIRM, P.A.
IMMIGRATION LAW GROUP
4602 IDS Center - Minneapolis, MN 55402
Phone: (612) 332-0082, Fax: (612) 332-8368

The Borene Law Firm, P.A., with highly experienced attorneys and staff members, provides worldwide professional legal services for all types of immigration and visa-related matters. The firm has broad experience with the application of immigration law and visa procedures on its clients' behalf. Its attorneys are active in international, national and regional leadership of the immigration bar and are frequent speakers and authors on immigration topics for professional and public groups. Over the past 18 years, the firm's attorneys have represented or advised thousands of immigration clients from every region of the world and more than 125 countries. Starting from a solid understanding of its clients' long- and short-term needs, the firm uses a resourceful and cost-effective approach to help clients meet their immigration goals.

The firm's business clients include:
•Fortune 500 companies
•International law firms
•International corporations
•Foreign investors
•Major hospitals and clinics
•Research universities
•Family-owned and small businesses
•Individual entrepreneurs

The firm's professional clients include:
•Business executives and managers
•Scientific and technical professionals—research, computer and engineering professionals
•Health care professionals—physicians, nurses and allied health care professionals
•Educators—professors, teachers, administrators and other education professionals
•Prominent public figures, artists, entertainers and athletes
•Other professionals and skilled workers

The firm's individual clients include:
•Relatives of United States citizens and permanent residents—family-based immigration projects
•Citizenship applicants
•Temporary visitors to the United States

The Borene Law Firm, P.A., has provided immigration representation and special counsel to many corporations and world-leading organizations including Mayo Clinic; Mayo Foundation; Medtronic; University of Minnesota; ACT/American College Testing; Saint Paul Pioneer Press; Schwan's Sales Enterprises; GMAC/Residential Funding Corporation; North Dakota State University; Luther College; Meier Tool & Engineering; SIFCO Custom Machining Company; DataMedica; ViroMed Laboratories; Jones Ranch; Richfield Bank and Trust; and many other employers large and small.

LIST OF SELECTED LEADING MINNESOTA ATTORNEYS
PRACTICING IN THE AREAS OF

Arts, Entertainment & Sports Law
Bankruptcy Law: Individual
Employment Law: Individual
Felony & Misdemeanor Criminal Defense Law
Immigration Law: Individual

The following attorneys were selected by their peers as Leading Minnesota Attorneys in one or more of the areas of law listed above. Many attorneys are selected in more than one area. For a complete list of all current Leading Minnesota Attorneys, visit our Web site at www.lawlead.com

Kenneth J. Abdo
Jeff P. Anderson
Jeffrey R. Anderson
Craig W. Andresen
Robert D. Aronson
David Ayers
Corey Ayling
Ian Traquair Ball
Michelle Barrette
Thomas E. Bauer
K. Scott Belfry
Stephen R. Bergerson
Charles A. Bird
Andrew S. Birrell
Bailey W. Blethen
Joseph P. Bluth
Jean M. Boler
Scott M. Borene
Richard L. Breitman
John C. Brink
Frederic Bruno
Don L. Bye
Peter A. Cahill
Allan Caplan

Colia F. Ceisel
Edward J. Cleary
Michael J. Colich
Stephen W. Cooper
Gregg M. Corwin
Michael F. Cromett
James J. Dailey
Laura J. Danielson
Lisa D. Dejoras
Michael J. Dolan
Karim G. El-Ghazzawy
Daniel A. Eller
Karen Ellingson
Kathryn Engdahl
Paul Engh
Phillip F. Fishman
Joseph S. Friedberg
Barbara J. Gislason
Stephen D. Gordon
Earl P. Gray
Malin D. Greenberg
Lesley M. Guyton
Bruce H. Hanley
Charles L. Hawkins

Douglas A. Hedin
Stuart R. Hemphill
Daniel J. Heuel
Donald E. Horton
Michael J. Iannacone
Jerome B. Ingber
Peter Irvine
Debra Kass Orenstein
James H. Kaster
David C. Keegan
Thomas M. Kelly
Wayne A. Kenas
Paul A. Kief
Gerald T. Laurie
John C. Levy
Anne Lewis
Thomas W. Lies
Calvin L. Litsey
Patrick A. Lowther
Kevin A. Lund
John W. Lundquist
Robert G. Malone
James H. Manahan
Seymour J. Mansfield

Patricia G. Mattos
William J. Mauzy
William J. Mavity
Samuel A. McCloud
Saiko Y. McIvor
Susan A. McKay
Nancy Miller
Gordon G. Mohr
Daniel M. Mohs
Joanne J. Mullen
Howard S. Myers
Thomas M. Neuville
Donald H. Nichols
Maurice W. O'Brien
Teresa Patton
Richard L. Pemberton
David T. Peterson
Jack L. Prescott
John W. Provo
Charles J. Ramstad

Larry G. Rapoport
Phillip S. Resnick
Jeffrey B. Ring
Donna L. Roback
David G. Roston
Andrea F. Rubenstein
James G. Ryan
Daniel M. Satorius
William M. Schade
Peter J. Schmitz
John Sheehy
Thomas H. Shiah
Kevin J. Short
Robert Sicoli
Alf Sivertson
Louis N. Smith
Stephen J. Snyder
Paul C. Sprenger
Susan B. Stingley
Elizabeth Storaasli

John H. Stout
Jerry Strauss
Marshall H. Tanick
Elizabeth A. Thompson
Douglas W. Thomson
Paul R. Thorwaldsen
John D. Undem
Stephen R. Van Drake
Philip G. Villaume
Karla R. Wahl
Robert M. Wallner
Mark S. Wernick
James C. Wicka
Douglas J. Williams
Peter B. Wold
Scott W. Wright
Richard T. Wylie
Lloyd Zimmerman